TRANS MEDICINE

Trans Medicine

The Emergence and Practice of Treating Gender

stef m. shuster

NEW YORK UNIVERSITY PRESS

New York

NEW YORK UNIVERSITY PRESS
New York
www.nyupress.org

References to Internet websites (URLs) were accurate at the time of writing. Neither the author nor New York University Press is responsible for URLs that may have expired or changed since the manuscript was prepared.

Library of Congress Cataloging-in-Publication Data
Names: shuster, stef m., author.
Title: Trans medicine : the emergence and practice of treating gender / stef m. shuster.
Description: [New York, New York] : New York University Press, [2021] | Includes bibliographical references and index.
Identifiers: LCCN 2020047263 | ISBN 9781479845378 (hardback) | ISBN 9781479899371 (paperback) | ISBN 9781479842810 (ebook) | ISBN 9781479836291 (ebook)
Subjects: LCSH: Transgender people—Medical care—United States. | Gender-nonconforming people—Medical care—United States. | Health services accessibility—United States. | Right to health—United States. | Medical ethics—United States.
Classification: LCC RA564.9.T73 S48 2021 | DDC 362.1086/7—dc23
LC record available at https://lccn.loc.gov/2020047263

New York University Press books are printed on acid-free paper, and their binding materials are chosen for strength and durability. We strive to use environmentally responsible suppliers and materials to the greatest extent possible in publishing our books.

Manufactured in the United States of America

10 9 8 7 6 5 4 3 2 1

Also available as an ebook

CONTENTS

GLOSSARY

AMERICAN PSYCHIATRIC ASSOCIATION (APA): The professional association for US-based psychiatrists that publishes the *Diagnostic and Statistical Manual of Mental Disorders.*

CLINICAL GUIDELINES: Guidelines represent recommendations for medical decision-making. They are often supported by scientific evidence and informed by a systematic review of evidence and medical consensus. They outline a sequence of steps a provider is encouraged to take in the diagnosis and prognosis of illness and disease.

DIAGNOSTIC AND STATISTICAL MANUAL OF MENTAL DISORDERS (DSM): Published by the APA to offer standard criteria for diagnosing and classifying mental health disorders.

EVIDENCE-BASED MEDICINE (EBM): A model of medicine that that uses scientific evidence to help standardize medical decision-making. Typically evaluates evidence as a hierarchy, with randomized controlled trials at the top and case studies at the bottom.

GENDER-AFFIRMING CARE: I use this term to refer to all interventions that fall under trans medicine including therapy, hormone therapy (e.g., estrogen or testosterone), and surgery (e.g., vaginoplasty or chest masculinization surgery). Some may use the similar, but less agentic, phrase "sex reassignment surgery" or "gender reassignment surgery."

INTERNATIONAL CLASSIFICATION OF DISEASES (ICD): Published by the World Health Organization to offer standard criteria for diagnosing and classifying all mental and physical health issues. It is also used internationally for insurance reimbursement systems and gathering morbidity and mortality statistics.

NONBINARY: This term references people who identify with a gender that is beyond the binary categories of woman or man (e.g., genderqueer).

TARGET GENDER: I use this term to refer to the gender that one is transitioning toward.

TRANS: I use this term in an all-encompassing way to refer to people whose gender identities differ from their gender assignment at birth. This may include binary trans people (i.e., trans women or trans men) and nonbinary people (i.e. genderqueer or genderfluid people). I do not assume that all trans people seek medical interventions.

TRANSSEXUAL: This term was used more frequently from the 1950s through the early 2000s to refer to trans people who sought medical interventions for a gender transition.

WORLD HEALTH ORGANIZATION (WHO): An international organization that publishes the *International Classification of Diseases*.

WORLD PROFESSIONAL ASSOCIATION FOR TRANSGENDER HEALTH (WPATH): An international organization of medical professionals that created the first guidelines (referred to as the Standards of Care) for trans medicine in 1979. They continue to revise the guidelines every few years.

PREFACE

Arriving in Iowa in 2007 to begin my PhD program in sociology, I began asking various units on the University of Iowa's campus what resources were available for trans people, especially in health services. Iowa City is a small college town that many local residents describe as a liberal bubble in the middle of a cornfield. The UI has a teaching hospital and does not mirror other small cities that face a scarcity of medical providers. But it was incredibly difficult to find any providers who wanted to work with me, let alone those willing to do so. I had identified as nonbinary and trans for quite a few years before arriving in Iowa City, but up until I accepted a spot in the PhD program, my income had been tenuous, and I was unable to access any gender-affirming healthcare.

The early 2000s were a time in trans medicine when few providers were aware of the existence of trans people, and even less aware of nonbinary people, even though the rise of hormone therapy and surgical interventions began in the middle of the 20th century. The handful of providers of trans medicine in Iowa City followed the clinical guidelines from a literal interpretation, which meant that they requested I undergo six months of therapy before I could begin taking hormones or find a surgeon who would work with me. This was confusing to me, as a young adult who at that point in my life was financially independent and beginning to work on a doctoral degree. These requests also felt infantilizing. But, like many other trans and nonbinary people with limited options, I decided it was worth it to comply with these requests. I was fortunate to find a therapist who met my skepticism about the gatekeeping prevalent in trans medicine with an open mind. In fact, he changed my orientation on the value of therapy in general. Within a year I had gender-affirming top surgery. A few years beyond that, I also began taking testosterone with a provider in Iowa City who, like my therapist, practiced medicine from a gender-affirming stance.

Around the same time, I had been heavily involved in healthcare organizing and advocacy with a group that I started, TransCollaborations. This was both a community and a campus advocacy group that offered workshops across campus and in the community, touching on any and all aspects of life that trans people negotiate. We brought speakers to Iowa City, held zine-making parties, and organized on behalf of trans people in healthcare services—generalist, specialist, sexual assault services, and mental health. Through this organization, I developed several close working relationships with medical providers. What I heard in the workshops and planning sessions was that providers felt unequipped to work in trans medicine, anxious about making decisions, and urgently in need of information and evidence so that they could do their work with more confidence. This was an early preview for me to learn about the perspectives that providers brought into their work, the kinds of questions they had about how to work with trans people, and the uncertainty they grappled with.

In 2012, I was unaware of anyone who had brought a sociological perspective to the medical provider side of trans medicine. The curious fascination that the social scientific community has had with *how* people undergo gender transitions felt like an exhausted (and exhausting) topic. My healthcare advocacy work with TransCollaborations and being engaged in conversations with health providers in the Iowa City area served as the catalyst to shift the focus of this project, which began with interviewing trans people, to the medical establishment.

I had my own uncertainties about how medical sociologists and sociologists of gender might respond to this "weird" area of study. The 2008 recession brought new anxieties into the academic job market, where "playing it safe" was the typical advice offered to early-career scholars. In spite of these concerns, I felt compelled to take the risk. In flipping the lens onto the medical community to shift the focus of study on them, rather than trans people, I wanted to find out how providers make sense of "treating" gender in medicine, given that medical decision-making is typically oriented toward diagnosing illnesses and treating diseases.

These questions led to over three years of research in archival collections of mid-20th-century letters of correspondence between providers, as well as interviewing providers across the US and observing them presenting to each other in trans-specific healthcare conferences. Most of the data was collected between 2012 and 2015, and eventually formed the basis of this book project.

Introduction

A young medical doctor tentatively raises her hand in a darkened auditorium that holds three hundred of her peers and asks the panelists
at a transgender healthcare conference how they make decisions about
enabling or blocking access to hormones for their trans patients. The
young doctor continues to reflect upon how she struggles the most with
patients who are nonbinary-identified, meaning that their gender identities are neither woman nor man, but somewhere outside or beyond
these categories. One panelist who has worked in trans medicine for
over 20 years chuckles, leans into the microphone, and explains that
"It's sort of like Spidey-sense. You know? [*pause*] You sort of have to
feel it out." The audience nervously laughs while nodding their heads
in agreement that when handling uncertainty in medical decision-
making with trans people, one must trust one's gut instinct or so-called
Spidey-sense.

Sitting in the audience, I was taken aback at this exchange. All of the
training that medical providers receive in internships, in residency programs, and in the years beyond medical school advances their knowledge and confidence about offering the best medical treatment possible.
They look to published research when they are presented with ambiguous cases. They call each other on the phone or knock on their colleagues' doors when they are unsure how to diagnose or treat patients.
To maintain their licenses to practice medicine, they are also expected to
continue their education through regularly attending conferences. These
cumulative activities help providers develop a gut instinct about making
medical decisions when managing uncertainty.[1] In medical emergencies,
relying on gut instinct helps providers quickly make decisions, which
can become a life-or-death matter for their patients.[2] But when con-

fronted with uncertainty in medical decisions that are not quite so immediate, what factors are at play in developing and using gut instinct?[3]

Historical and ethnographic investigation consistently reaffirms that multiple mechanisms exist that dictate the justification for refusing or allowing trans interventions by providers. What is less understood is how informal and subjective evidence becomes crystallized, established, and perpetuated as providers accumulate knowledge and experience in gender-affirming interventions. This book begins as an acknowledgment that providers of trans medicine have an established authority over gender, and asks, How has medical authority over gender happened? What has become normal and legitimate through decades of practice in trans medicine? And what are the consequence of these trends for trans medicine and the medical establishment more broadly? This book is an effort to move toward these answers and find opportunities for a more inclusive and just healthcare system.

After spending over three years examining hundreds of letters of correspondence between health providers working in the middle of the 20th century, interviewing 23 providers who work with trans patients, and observing providers in trans-specific healthcare conferences across the US, it became clear to me that when trans people show up in their clinics, what providers describe experiencing is like an existential crisis. Medical providers are rarely trained in offering gender-affirming interventions such as hormone therapy.[4] Trans healthcare is mentioned, if at all, on the one diversity day that occurs during a typical medical student's education.[5] This lack of direct training in trans medical interventions raises a considerable amount of uncertainty for residents. Even beyond the formal years of residency programs, most providers have not had enough hands-on experience or opportunities to establish a body of medical knowledge to draw upon, as they have in other areas of their practice. As they describe it, Spidey-sense helps providers resolve the dissonance between how they are taught to think about and treat illness and disease and the reality that they are not trained explicitly in gender.

While there are ongoing debates in medical sociology about how much or little providers are trained to deal with uncertainty, these providers of trans medicine are confronted with it every step of the way in their work with trans people. Exacerbating the uncertainty is the combination of a dearth of experience and little existing evidence that, in their own words, helps them figure out how to work with trans people or make decisions in gender-affirming care.[6] This situation challenges providers' sense of themselves as medical experts.

Trans medicine offers a lens through which we can understand how medicine is a place where science and values meet. Many providers eschew the idea that their personal belief systems matter in medicine, as science and experience are the foundations of medical decision-making. Nonbinary people who seek access to gender-affirming interventions amplify the uncertainties that providers have about trans medicine.[7] Genderqueer, genderfluid, agender (and many more genders) people, those we might understand as in some way understanding themselves as nonbinary-gendered people, upend the medical knowledge that has begun to accumulate in trans medicine. Where previously it was assumed that people seeking access to gender-transition-related care sought to transition from woman to man, or man to woman, the goal of treatment in working with trans patients shifts when the person seeking treatment does not desire to maintain a binary gender expression. Providers, like most professionals, sometimes have difficulty keeping up with social changes as their knowledge and practice habits become routinized, making it challenging to find alternate pathways to refresh knowledge or break from traditional ways of thinking about a topic or group of people.[8]

Further amplifying these challenges are the expectations that their professional associations and patients have of them to make well-informed decisions about the health and well-being of their trans patients. In response, some double down on their authority, insisting that they are the providers and patients should follow their orders. This group of providers hold a principled view that medical authority helps to create order in a decision-making process that, from their perspective, feels disordered. Other providers are more flexible and describe working, but sometimes stumbling, their way toward clarity in what a best practice might look like. They seek to find a middle ground between patients' needs and medical authority. In the process, many of these providers find that they learn more about gender and the intimate spaces of the lives of patients who seek their help in gender transitions. The historical contexts that shape their assumptions and knowledge remain important to contemporary trans medicine in how the "treatment" of gender is understood by the medical establishment and in the uncertainties they continue to experience in when to block or initiate gender-affirming interventions. How providers negotiate these intimate features of trans medicine is the heart of what this book is about.

Evidence in Medical Decision-Making

A central reason why providers experience so much uncertainty—both historically and currently—in trans medicine is that they feel like they have little evidence to draw from. In medicine, evidence takes varied forms. It can include data from research-driven activities such as clinical trials on the effects of pharmaceutical interventions or studies detailing the outcomes of medical procedures.[9] Clinical guidelines or diagnostic categories offer providers guidance in recognizing symptoms and recommended steps for treatment plans.[10] Evidence can also be culled from clinical experience and learning on the job.[11] And, as the opening scene makes clear, gut instinct sometimes functions as evidence, too.

The mere fact that providers ritually described concerns about the lack of evidence signals something sociologically important about the contexts that shape providers who make this claim. Clearly there is evidence in trans medicine. For example, there are many studies published on the efficacy of surgical techniques or the effects of hormone therapy on trans people's bodies, such as the amount of testosterone that trans men might use to achieve facial hair growth, fat redistribution, and the thickening of vocal cords that lowers one's voice.[12] The physicians I spoke with acknowledged these studies help them assess how much testosterone to prescribe. But these kinds of published results did little to help providers address how and when to initiate, continue, or block access to hormones or how to interact with trans patients in the clinic.

What providers are describing, then, when they say they lack evidence, is that from their perspective they do not think that they have the adequate tools to decide under what conditions it is acceptable to initiate or gatekeep gender-affirming interventions. As a result, these providers may be unintentionally engaging in trans exceptionalism,[13] where they perceive trans patients as so unique and different from cisgender patients that they have a difficult time importing evidence and their experience from other areas of medicine into their decision-making and interactions with trans patients.[14]

The case of trans medicine calls attention to broader trends in contemporary medicine. The rise in evidence-based medicine (EBM) in the 1990s fundamentally altered the landscape of medical decision-making and evaluations of evidence.[15] EBM refers to the "conscientious, explicit, and judicious use of the most current scientific evidence available for medical decision-making."[16] The medical community's hope has been that in using scientific evidence, variation in practices and decision-making would be alleviated. A key feature of EBM is that evidence is derived from a systematic review of existing literature to help construct best practices. One of the more contentious aspects of EBM is that it ranks evidence according to the reliability and verifiability of research, which communicates the idea that only some forms of evidence are valid.[17] Randomized controlled trials are at the top, and case studies are at the bottom, of this evidence hierarchy.[18]

A typical way that EBM manifests is through clinical guidelines, which are constructed as handbooks for providers to help inform medical practices and routinize everyday clinical decisions by using empirical evidence.[19] Guidelines empower providers to quickly assess legitimated knowledge and access guidance on making decisions. However, guidelines potentially restrict providers' activities by serving as sites of regulation by third parties, administrators, and legislators. For example, if a provider makes a decision on behalf of a patient's particular needs that is not aligned with the recommendations, they may not be reimbursed by insurance companies for the care delivered.[20] This puts pressure on providers to follow the guidelines, or manage them strategically, to conform to these outside pressures.[21]

Trans medicine has followed the rest of the medical establishment in turning toward EBM. An extraordinary amount of work has been undertaken to construct clinical guidelines and diagnostic tools for the assessment and treatment of trans identities. Over the last several decades, there has been a proliferation of these medical artifacts, which has been revered by some providers and leaders in the field as elevating the status of trans medicine.[22] As feminist science and technology studies scholar Rebecca Herzig noted, the mere mention of evidence affords a practice a sense of legitimacy, especially when couched in the rhetoric of scientific evidence.[23]

A puzzle emerges in the structure of medicine when looking at the guidelines and diagnostic criteria for emergent fields of medicine. As I will show, providers use the language of evidence in trans medicine for social reasons. There is little existing evidence in trans medicine that meets the gold standards for EBM.[24] This puts providers in a difficult position of defending their decision-making. Using the language of science shores up doubt about this contentious area of medicine, but other stakeholders including insurance companies and policy makers may not recognize such claims because the evidence that is privileged— clinical trials that sit at the top of a rigid evidence hierarchy—cannot be met in trans medicine. It would be unethical to conduct clinical trials. Trans and nonbinary people make up such a small group—with the best estimates suggesting between 0.4 to 0.6 percent of the total US population,[25] and those who can or choose to access medical interventions even smaller—that it would be impossible to obtain a randomized trial. Some providers of trans medicine also question how they can justify the decisions they make, when the evidence they seek—that which may help them grapple with a particular patient group that many know so little about—is lacking.[26] At the same time, the consensus of the US medical community, including many of the providers I interviewed, works within the principle that gender-affirming care is a basic human right and access to it helps alleviate health disparities among trans and non-binary people.[27]

Medical Expertise & Uncertainty

In healthcare domains, expertise is accrued from clinical experience and scientific research and translates into an expectation that providers know what they are doing and make informed decisions in caring for patients.[28] Without expertise, the status of an occupation declines and it becomes difficult for a working professional to carry out their job.[29] But what happens when one's expertise is untranslatable in new areas of medicine or there are disagreements about who should be able to claim expertise in a field? According to sociologist Andrew Abbott, professions use expertise to create jurisdictional boundaries for themselves. But when the boundaries for jurisdictional fields are murky, professions may battle over the same areas of work.[30] This is the situation in trans medicine, which has created conflict between mental and physical healthcare workers.

Although trans medical expertise began to accumulate and was dispersed among a handful of providers in the 1950s, there remains a disagreement on whether mental healthcare providers or physicians should primarily be responsible for decision-making in gender-affirming care.[31] The structure of trans medicine is diffused across areas of specialization. In physical healthcare, physicians, gynecologists, and endocrinologists primarily work with trans people in everyday medical encounters and provide trans-specific healthcare such as hormone therapy. In mental healthcare, counselors, psychologists, and psychiatrists work with trans people through everyday concerns, as well as for trans-specific therapy.

Each of these areas of medicine has a different set of assumptions about how to understand, define, and work within trans medicine. As a result, most providers of trans medicine experience a great deal of uncertainty, which is exacerbated by the fact that gender-affirming treatments are not the same as treating an illness or disease. Uncertainty, according to health scholar Merle Mishel, is "the inability to determine the meaning of illness-related events and occurs in situations where the decision-maker is unable to assign definitive values to objects or events. It results from the ambiguity, complexity, and unpredictability of illness or deficiency of information about one's illness and its consequences."[32] Many providers do not communicate the uncertainty about risks and benefits of treatments with their patients because admitting the unknown challenges a professional's ability to claim expertise.

Uncertainty is now understood as ubiquitous in medical decision-making and providers have a variety of ways to respond to it.[33] They can double down on their medical authority and hold themselves up as experts to alleviate concerns about their medical decision-making.[34] Providers can also work with their patients to find a middle ground when presented with uncertainty. In the field of neurogenetics, for example, providers often work within a context where there is little scientific evidence to support medical decision-making. To confront this situation, providers may turn to the client as an expert in co-constructing biomedical knowledge.[35] Health communications scholar Lucy Brookes-Howell found that genetic counselors, facing uncertainty, worked closely with clients to find a mutually constituted decision and accept the uncertainty of results from genetic tests.[36]

As providers of trans medicine explained in the interviews, they experienced diagnostic uncertainty, which asks providers to take what is known and make a best guess as to what is to come.[37] These providers are in a bind, as they are unable to anticipate "what is to come" except the hope that trans patients who access gender-affirming care will, overall, be in a better place than if they are denied care outright. However, sometimes the uncertainty that providers experience creates enough dissonance that in the efforts to quell it, they unintentionally perpetuate healthcare inequalities.

Medical Authority over Gender

Medical authority is conferred by evidence, experience, and expertise. Authority becomes fraught when evidence and experience are sparse. But how did providers acquire authority over gender itself? The durability of authority has been a remarkable feature of the medical establishment ever since the profession began to accumulate power through educational training programs, licensure, and professional associations in the 1800s.[38] Over the past several decades there have been calls to decentralize the authority of medical providers by shifting away from paternalistic care, which is colloquially referred to as a "doctor knows best" decision-making model, and toward patient-centered care.[39] Scholars who study the social aspects of medicine have conflicting accounts as to whether medical authority has increased or decreased in modern medicine.[40] But recent studies have identified how the profession of medicine absorbs challenges to authority by co-opting potentially transformative changes or demands for reform made by patient groups.[41] In studying trans medicine, we can learn a great deal about how providers negotiate their relationships with medical authority within these larger debates, and how medical authority has changed over time and in response to shifting norms surrounding medicine and gender.

Medicine has been an influential institution in creating medicalized understandings of gender.[42] "Medicalization" refers to the process of how non-medical problems become defined and treated as medical problems.[43] For example, "hysteria" was a medical label developed in the 1800s to categorize women who were perceived as irrational, sexually active, or not abiding by social norms as to how proper women should act.[44] As sociologist Peter Conrad has found studying the rise of medicalization in modern society, it has far-reaching effects in that providers adopt a medical framework to understand the problem, which elevates their authority to then "treat" the named problem with medical interventions.[45] In the case of hysteria, the medical community determined that the best course of treatment for hysterics was to send women to asylums or have a period of rest at home to settle their troubled minds.[46] Hysterics were removed from society and brought under the jurisdiction of medical authority.

The case of hysteria also shows how nonconformity to social norms troubles the medical establishment. Through labeling people or behavior as nonconforming, medical communities are empowered to establish and sustain cultural norms.[47] In the process, identities and bodies are placed under increased surveillance by the medical establishment.[48] For example, sociologist Elizabeth M. Armstrong interviewed women who drink alcohol while carrying a fetus to showcase how information about healthy pregnancies became a rallying cry for medical and scientific communities to control women's bodies in the name of protecting future generations.[49] Health information, Armstrong shows, is often presumed to be reflective of accumulated knowledge from the medical and scientific community. But the relationship between women who drink during pregnancy and the potential adverse effects on the fetus is not well researched. Instead, social ideas about the character of women who drink while pregnant influence medical communities' assumptions about how women should behave while pregnant, and these assumptions in turn become recognized as scientific facts. Thus, as Armstrong's work shows, medical and scientific communities do not simply observe and act on facts. Through medicalization, social ideas about bodies become accepted as scientific "facts," which, once categorized as such, are difficult to change, as they are filtered through social mores and become rooted in culturally accepted norms.

In trans medicine, the medicalization of gender has been routed through both mental and physical healthcare communities. These pathways to care are rooted in mid-20th-century understandings of who should treat trans people, and in what kind of "disordered" object is implied with treatment. Is the goal of treatment to bring the mind into alignment with the body, or to change one's body to bring relief to one's mental health state? Rather than taking a position on this debate, providers have operated from the tacit assumption that the best way forward in medical decision-making is to understand trans identification as a mental health issue *and* to work from a biomedical model of care. This has created a double-whammy effect of medicalization in trans people's lives as they are subject to both mental and physical healthcare providers' authority. Furthermore, in health encounters where the power differentials can be extreme between patient and provider, whose knowledge of gender matters and can alter the pathways to decision-making that providers and patients undergo. I argue throughout this book that how gender is defined, and by whom, reflects dominant norms about proper gender identification and bodily displays.

providing care with no external influences

Telling Stories with Data

To address the questions that frame this book in how providers negotiate uncertainty, given their perceptions of lacking evidence to make decisions, which presented a challenge to their claims of expertise, I used a multi-sited research design. Building on the scholarship in feminist ethnographic methods, I tell a full story not only of the historical contexts of trans medicine, but of how those contexts shaped and continue to shape contemporary realities for medical providers.

I began my research by examining letters of correspondence between providers working in the middle of the 20th century. These letters were found in the archives of the Kinsey Institute, which houses a number of collections and artifacts from the mid-20th-century biologist and sexologist Alfred C. Kinsey, along with donations of other objects related to sexuality that people have made over the years. Documents from scientists and healthcare providers reflect scientific and medical discourse on trans people and how providers made decisions regarding whether a person was eligible for gender-affirming medical interventions. A story began to emerge through this archival work about the assumptions that medical providers brought into their work with trans people. It would take interviews with providers, however, to puzzle through how, while we think much has changed in trans medicine, the same frames continue to inform the structuring of trans medicine and the uncertainty that providers experience.

I conducted 23 in-depth interviews with therapists and physicians from a variety of specialties and theoretical orientations, locations across the United States, and work settings. I asked broad categories of questions that included providers' backgrounds in medicine and their professional association memberships, the model of care used, and their experiences working with trans clients. I also asked providers to share with me their typical, and then ideal, patient intake process, how they made decisions to block or enable access interventions, what flags stood out to them to block interventions, and how they grappled with challenges. The interviews helped illustrate how contemporary medical perspectives are crafted from the assumptions of those providers working in trans medicine in the middle of the 20th century and the continued challenges of this medical field. But there were still gaps in my own understanding. I didn't feel like I had the full story.

Conducting observations at healthcare conferences helped me understand how providers teach each other how to work with patient populations in a less scripted environment. I took notes on the information that providers presented in workshops that appeared in the medical education track of the conference, the questions that conference attendees asked, and how panelists responded to these questions. Through these observations I realized that the public stories that providers told each other were somewhat different than the data from the interviews. In the interviews, providers offered many examples of uncertainty and not knowing the best practices in trans medicine. The healthcare conferences were replete with providers who directly addressed their uncertainties with each other and retold an overarching narrative of progress in trans medicine since the "dark years of the 1950s," as one conference workshop presenter suggested.

One last data collection strategy helped round out my understanding of the state of the field of trans medicine. Clinical guidelines, standards of care, and diagnostic criteria were a primary source of information that providers discussed using to help guide their decisions in trans medicine. Thus, it was clear to me that examining these documents was crucial because so many of the presenters in the trans healthcare conferences and the medical providers interviewed for this book invoked them. I examined the diagnostic criteria and clinical guidelines associated with trans medicine from several leading associations, including the American Psychiatric Association, the Endocrine Society, the World Professional Association for Trans Health, and the World Health Organization, and how they have changed over time. The analysis of these documents helped me understand how these various professional associations construct evidence in the diagnosis and prognosis of what is now referred to as gender dysphoria, and the assumptions regarding gender that shape medical decision-making.

I use these data to tell different kinds of stories than those that have already been told. My analysis of data is informed by a blending of sociology of knowledge with feminist science and technology studies perspectives. As sociologists Peter Berger and Thomas Luckmann suggest in their now classic work on the construction of reality, a sociologist of knowledge deals with "not only the empirical variety of knowledge . . . but also with the processes by which any body of knowledge comes to be socially established as reality."[50] This means that I examine the perspectives of medical providers—past and present—and carefully consider what gendered assumptions they bring into their work and the contexts that shape those assumptions and have lasting impacts on their perspectives. In this way, I do not take scientific and medical knowledge at face value. Instead, I approach it as situated knowledge that is contested, malleable, and contextualized by the historical, social, and cultural forces in which it emerged and is used by those in the medical establishment to "treat" gender.[51]

A Note on Changing Understandings of Sex and Gender

As historian Joan Scott reflects, "Those who would codify the meanings of words fight a losing battle, for words, like the ideas and things they are meant to signify, have a history."[52] For example, I use the term "trans" throughout the book, even in the historical chapters. I understand that this term did not come into use as an umbrella term to describe people whose gender expression and identities do not align with their sex assignment at birth until the 1990s.[53] I retain the original word choices of providers when quoting directly, but I use the all-encompassing "trans" to describe what was happening in both historical and contemporary trans medicine.

Sex, sexuality, and gender, and the words used to describe such categories, are in flux and are reflective of social, historical, and cultural contexts.[54] For anyone writing about the historical and contemporary landscapes of gender and medicine, this is a particularly difficult aspect to negotiate in how these terms are understood within the historical moments in which they are used and in how they shift over time.[55] Consider, for example, that before the Enlightenment period, human bodies were not medically differentiated by "female" and "male" categories. During this time, scientists observed differences in reproductive organs and genitals, but it was assumed that bodies were more similar than different and were not distinguished on the basis of difference. Historian Thomas Laqueur referred to this as the "one-sex" model and documented how scientists began to classify sex differences in response to massive political, economic, and cultural forces.[56] As a result, differences between female and male bodies shifted into causal explanations for why females should be subordinated to males.

The historical development of sex and gender can also be understood as one marked by medical and scientific communities using emergent knowledge and technologies to propagate ideas of normalcy. Biologist, historian, and feminist science studies scholar Anne Fausto-Sterling's work documented how, beginning in the 1800s, sex categories proliferated as medical and scientific communities began to study in earnest those whose reproductive organs and genitals were not aligned within a sexual dimorphic system. Instead of understanding this group, whom we would now refer to as intersex people, as representative of natural variation in sex, they regarded intersex people as abnormal. With the rise of statistics and ideas of a "population," distinctions between average or normal bodies were juxtaposed against the abnormal.[57] In response, medical communities sought to "correct" bodily differences through surgical interventions. *medical = correction mental = therapy*

By the early 20th century, scientific and medical communities worked fervently to create taxonomical classifications of sexual variation. Central in these conversations was Magnus Hirschfeld, a sexologist in Germany who advocated the idea that all people varied on a continuum from "true male" to "true female."[58] A more expansive definition of "female" and "male" was contained within this continuum that was based on sexual organs, physical characteristics, sex drive, and the emotional characteristics of people. Hirschfeld also had wide-reaching impacts on the development of trans medicine in the United States. He mentored Harry Benjamin, a young endocrinologist who moved to the US in the 1940s and became a well-known provider for people we now understand as trans. While Benjamin used his knowledge of hormones to help transsexuals achieve the secondary sex characteristics of the "opposite" sex, other researchers were inspired by psychological understandings of human behavior and identity. Through studying intersex people, sexologist John Money and his research team coined the term "gender role." They popularized the idea that sex and gender categories were separate; sex was perceived as biologically indicated physical attributes such as anatomy or chromosomes and assumed to be fixed, while gender was psychologically rooted and more malleable.[59] As medical providers and scientists began to use finer-grained distinctions between trans people (as those who had gender identities misaligned with their bodies) and intersex people (as those who had ambiguously sexed bodies), they also began to differentiate their language and practices to work in distinct ways with these populations.

In tracing the complicated unfolding of variation in sex and gender over time and in relation to changing knowledge and authority over sex and gender, my sincere hope is not to make this account reductive. But what I do hope the reader can see through this condensed rendering of complicated histories is that the development of the term "transgender" must be understood within the medical and scientific community's investment in bringing order to perceived biological disorder. Furthermore, developments about bodies in medical and scientific knowledge often occur during moments of social upheaval.[60] The medical and scientific community's concerns with normalizing difference are not unique to trans medicine. In seeking to normalize, fix, or control difference, even when unintentional and reflective of current definitions of sex and gender, medical and scientific knowledge can be used against bodies to mandate compliance to social norms surrounding proper bodily comportment and displays.[61] How sex and gender are understood has lasting consequences in the lives of people who are rendered the object of inquiry and intervention by medical and scientific communities.

Book Overview

Part I of the book uses archival research from the Kinsey Institute to examine the historical contexts in the middle of the 20th century that laid the groundwork for contemporary trans medicine in the US. Chapter 1 examines how, with few trans patients during this time period and even fewer providers who worked in this medical area, providers faced accusations from those in the broader medical profession that they were "quacks." To establish their credibility, they instituted a set of criteria for sorting through worthy patients that mandated normative gender expression. During this time, providers placed an extraordinary emphasis on normalizing trans people's bodies and experiences. Those patients whose gender closely aligned with traditional ideology were more readily granted access to hormone therapy and surgical interventions. Trans people also had to demonstrate that they were model citizens in their employment and sexual desires. As such, social fitness became a litmus test for who was considered a worthy patient.

Chapter 2 traces how therapists became a central part of trans medicine. Around the 1960s, physicians realized they needed therapists to help assess whether a patient seeking gender-affirming care was "truly" trans or delusional. Legitimacy wars erupted between therapists and physicians, and between psychologists and psychiatrists, as each sought to establish themselves as the leading authorities in trans medicine. Psychiatrists aligned their skill set with their scientific training and began crafting diagnostic assessments to aid physicians. Psychologists leaned on their expertise in talk therapy to establish their expertise. Eventually, they began to work together to create agreed-upon protocols and increase their legitimacy by presenting a united front. By the end of the 1970s, physicians and therapists began working together in a team approach. Together, they agreed that trans people should be gender conforming, free from familial constraints, passive, and model citizens to be considered worthy of medical interventions.

In part II, I consider how the historical legacies of legitimacy wars, uncertainty, and using medical authority to treat gender continue to shape contemporary trans medicine. In chapter 3, I explore how contemporary providers have shifted their attention to constructing formal and informal evidence as a way to bolster the legitimacy of trans medicine. Evidence-based medicine (EBM) emerged in the late 1980s to bring a stronger scientific base into medical decision-making. Many providers in trans medicine have followed suit, heralding EBM and the creation of documents such as clinical guidelines and diagnostic tools as solutions to problems that plagued trans medicine in the past. Paradoxically, when we look beneath the surface of these documents, the evidence that is cited often does not meet the standard for reliable and valid scientific evidence. I consider how instead they are used to bolster the legitimacy of contemporary trans medicine. They are symbolic of the assumptions made about proper gender transitions. I also examine how providers construct informal evidence to further solidify their claims to authority over gender itself.

With the precarious way in which evidence has been established in trans medicine, and ongoing disputes among providers about the clinical guidelines and diagnostic criteria, there is an incredible amount of uncertainty. Chapter 4 draws from interviews and observations of healthcare conferences to examine how providers strategically use the clinical guidelines to alleviate uncertainty. Some used the rhetoric of EBM and closely followed clinical guidelines to contain uncertainty. Others flexibly interpreted the guidelines to embrace uncertainty. These findings raise questions about the effectiveness of EBM and guidelines in medical decision-making, and the pragmatic ways in which providers attempt to use the same strategies as they may in other medical arenas to respond to uncertainty.

Medical expertise is premised on clinical experience and scientific evidence. Many providers who work in trans medicine, though, have little clinical experience or scientific evidence to draw from to help guide medical decisions. These features of trans medicine directly conflict with expectations surrounding professional expertise. Using observations of trans healthcare conferences and interviews, in chapter 5 I examine how providers construct expertise, and the strategies they use to negotiate challenges to their expertise. Self-assured experts leverage the language of science and clinical guidelines to bolster their authority and claims to expertise. They shift their own uncertainty onto an expectation that trans people should demonstrate infallible certainty about gender-affirming interventions. Not all providers were invested in establishing expertise through authority. Uncertain experts acknowledged that they did not have the expertise in trans medicine that they have in other areas of their medical practice. As a result, they relinquished some control to their patients and, in the process, redefined the basic premise upon which medical expertise is built.

I conclude *Trans Medicine* by examining how a small but growing group of providers are rethinking the treatment of gender. Since its emergence, trans medicine has been fraught with professional landmines. But the providers I interviewed found joy in their work in spite of the challenges that besiege trans medicine. They teach us how the lasting legacy of oppression in trans medicine and efforts toward gender normalization is not insurmountable. These providers acknowledged that their work in addressing inequities is not complete. There are lasting challenges in trans medicine. For example, the uncertainty in medical decision-making that permeates trans medicine also raises questions about recent trends in evidence-based medicine as the gold standard for which all medical practices should strive. Additionally, the marginalization of trans medicine by the broader medical community implies that they are "off the hook" in working with trans people. This way of thinking presents problems for trans people when they interface with other medical providers and seek medical treatment outside of trans-specific concerns. It also makes it difficult for providers who work with trans people to find resources when atypical situations arise or when they need to refer their patients to other providers.

Rather than siloing trans people and trans medicine into a "specialty" track, all healthcare providers need to be properly trained in working with trans people—which would have spillover effects in more adequately meeting the needs of all patients, learning to work within gender variance, and avoiding perpetuating healthcare inequities.

PART I

Historical Contexts of Trans Medicine, 1950s–1970s

1

Creating Worthy Patients, 1950–1970

Historians who have detailed the early development of trans medicine often begin with Christine Jorgensen's story in the 1950s, as she was one of the first transsexuals to become internationally known through wide-scale coverage in mass media.[1] Captivating the attention of everyday readers, Jorgensen's story tantalized the general public, and the question of how a man could become a woman was a subject of lively conversation and curious fascination. Presenting as a softly feminine, put-together, middle-class war veteran and heterosexual woman, Jorgensen offered post–World War II society a close look into the triumphs of the scientific community's expanding knowledge about sex categories.[2] Americans were invested in restabilizing social life after the upheavals that the war brought into the intimate spaces of US households. With economic recovery efforts underway, and government incentive programs to help predominately young white families attain a middle-class life through home financing, mid-20th-century US life demanded that white middle-class women leave the factories to take care of the household while men returned to work.[3] As such, the 1950s are often upheld as a golden era for the traditional family household and gender relations.

In concert with the ideology of traditional gender roles and economic expansion, the public's trust in scientific and medical communities to solve social and biological ills was a prominent feature of mid-20th-century US life. Pharmaceutical, technological, and surgical innovations were heralded by the public. Operating within a "doctor knows best" paternalistic model of medicine, medical providers enjoyed a considerable amount of authority in medical decision-making in their clinical encounters with patients. The American Medical Association's consolidated power through increased licensing requirements, developments in areas of specialization, and expansion of its professional reach augmented the authority of medical providers.[4] These massive changes in broader society and the medical profession heavily influenced advancements in the science of sex and gender in the middle of the 20th century and shaped how medical providers understood, worked with, and researched transsexual patients.[5] Of particular concern was the normalization of transsexual bodies and experience.[6]

During this early era of what we now understand as trans medicine, providers who were compelled to enter, as one endocrinologist described it, this "brave new frontier of untrodden medicine" were conflicted. On the one hand, they wanted to help their patients, whom they also perceived as severely troubled individuals whose claims to being transsexuals were understood as symptomatic of delusional thinking.[7] On the other, they were excited by the prospect of being on the forefront of a new terrain of medical innovation and knowledge. As they began to accumulate knowledge about this developing area of medicine, the small handful of endocrinologists and physicians in the US who were willing to work with trans people faced criticism from their peers, who contested the idea that medically intervening in the lives of transsexuals was appropriate. To shelter themselves from colleagues' critiques that they were quacks, medical providers began to extensively correspond with each other—and often with the recognized authority in transsexual medicine, Harry Benjamin—and establish a shared understanding of transsexuals.

By instituting a set of normative guidelines, transsexuals were perceived as untrustworthy unless they acquiesced to a battery of medical tests and lengthy inquiries about their personal lives. Whether they chose or refused to comply, trans people were subject to being labeled, as one surgeon suggested in the early 1960s, "liars, deviants, and morally corrupt."[8] As I will show, the medical establishment's expectations for transsexuals became increasingly stringent over the 1960s, which helped to consolidate their authority in this emergent area of medicine. To sort out credible patients, the medical and scientific community sought as-surances that trans people would be able to successfully live in their tar-get gender. As I argue in this chapter, "successful" was defined in rigid ways that ultimately set up many trans people for denial of care if they were unable to fulfill the medical and scientific community's expecta-tions for gender conformity, heterosexual desire, stable jobs, and no in-terest in raising children. In sum, in a short amount of time between the 1950s and 1970s, medical and scientific communities created a shared knowledge base for filtering out trans people who could not be upheld as model citizens, and who were therefore perceived as unworthy of receiv-ing access to gender-affirming medical interventions.

The Quackery Quagmire

Leaving behind the country-doctor past—where any layperson could peddle their goods, potions, and miracle cures on the streets without any credentialing or verification from a regulatory agency—over the 19th century and into the 20th, medicine became recognized as a pro-fessionalized career through the establishment of medical education programs and licensure.[9] With the development and growth of the American Medical Association (AMA), the professional power of the medical community became further concentrated.[10] Without the sup-port of the AMA, some medical practices and interventions fell by the wayside, in favor of those procedures that had currency in the medical community. As sociologist Terri Winnick's research on the establish-ment of complementary and alternative medicine has demonstrated, the development of professional power to solidify the border between quackery and "real" medicine often coincides with claims to science and the use of empirical evidence. Simply laying claim to medical interven-tions backed by science legitimated 19th-century providers (previously referred to as allopaths).[11] Once medical schools were established as credible among the medical community, the state intervened by recog-nizing them as legitimate, affording them protection and credentialing, while also passing licensing laws to further support recognized doctors and medical practices.[12] Those providers who could not pass professional muster were subject to regulation by the federal government and the loss of their license to practice medicine.

The mid-20th century, in particular, has been described as the "golden age" of doctoring, as medical innovation and pharmaceutical knowledge were at a peak and trust in the medical profession was at a high among the general public.[13] In this era, scientific innovation and medical breakthroughs were celebrated as indicators of American superiority and intellectual rigor. But there was a threshold for innovation, and a fine line between quackery and medical discovery. Within these contexts of mass mobilization by the medical community to assert their expertise, the small handful of providers willing to work with trans people in the 1950s worried among themselves that the broader medical community did not favorably view what they were doing. As Harry Benjamin, an endocrinologist who had clinics in New York and San Francisco and became a well-known trusted figure in hormone therapy, reflected,

> I can't tell you how many of my fellows have called me aside for a heart-to-heart talk on this business of converting transsexuals. These, in every case, were friends of mine who had my interest at heart and who were worried about the gossip surrounding me and my office as a result of this type of work.[14]

Some providers feared that their medical licenses would be revoked. Both the general public and the scientific community had a fascination with trans people as a curious oddity. But there was no consensus that providers should medically intervene in the lives, and on the bodies, of trans people. This lack of consensus conflicted with the broader trends in medicine, where providers earnestly sought to professionalize medicine by casting out any practice or practitioner who did not uphold the status quo. "Sex-change surgeries," as they were referred to in the mid-20th century, did not fit this standard. Building on the earlier work of sexologists and the emergent area of endocrinology, most of the providers working with trans people during this time were endocrinologists or other physicians. While excited about this emergent area of medicine, they needed to assure those in the broader medical profession that they were not quacks for engaging in experimental medicine for a population of people regarded as unstable, delusional, and, in the words of one physician, "downright crazy."[15] Letters from doctors to Harry Benjamin suggested that some in the medical profession believed that medically intervening in the lives of trans people was immoral. As one of the only US-based surgeons working with trans people in the late 1950s shared in a letter to Benjamin, "I do wish we had a hospital available in which I could operate upon these patients without criticism. The present attitude of our fellow physicians toward this problem is pretty terrible to buck."[16]

Others in the medical community were concerned that a medical provider who considered working with trans people must, like their patients, be delusional.[17] As Benjamin reflected to a surgeon,

> I am strongly reminded of this connection of the attitude of the medical profession 50 years ago against a doctor who tried to change the shape of a nose. He was considered an outright quack. The day will come, I feel confident, when the alteration of secondary sex characteristics will be a perfectly legitimate field of medicine, and perhaps even a specialty.[18]

Without support from their colleagues, medical providers also faced the possibility of legal liability. As one physician wrote to the Erickson Educational Foundation, an organization founded in the 1960s to support research on transsexualism, "We need better legal protection for a surgeon who operates on a transsexual. A patient could conceivably change her mind and sue the doctor for mayhem."[19] And, as another surgeon shared, "I am being threatened by a paranoic [sic] patient whom you once saw years ago and refused to operate. Of course, he is a mental case, and probably pretty hopeless. He wants to sue me for not operating on him. Nice state of affairs, isn't it?"[20] The historical record does not suggest that many trans people sought legal mechanisms for asserting their right to gender-affirming care, as they wanted to avoid the legal system out of fears of being arrested for masquerading.[21]

Already on the books during wartime efforts, mayhem laws protected the government's interests by punishing individuals who willingly removed their limbs to avoid military service.[22] While they were initially conceived as a stopgap for military service members, as historians Susan Stryker and Nikki Sullivan suggest, mayhem laws were concerning to medical providers who agreed to perform trans-specific surgeries.[23] Using the legal definitions for "mayhem" as purposeful bodily harm, some in the medical community questioned whether trans medical surgeries might be legally interpreted as undermining an otherwise healthy person's body. If the state began prosecuting medical providers, it would undermine this growing area of medical innovation in the science of sex and gender.

In response to professional, public, and state pressures to clarify this "whole business of working with transsexuals," providers faced an incredible amount of uncertainty about how to work with transsexual patients who showed up in their clinics requesting access to surgical and hormonal interventions.[24] To establish credibility among their peers, the broader public, and the government, they began to frame their work within the spirit of scientific research. As Benjamin wrote in a letter about someone in Casablanca who was establishing a name for himself for performing trans surgery,

I am happy to know there is someone in Casablanca sufficiently venturesome to launch upon this type of work. I hope that he is well-equipped and will do a good job. I do not know this doctor, his background or experience. We ourselves have had so many surprises and have learned so much in doing these types of cases. My letter to him is sort of a feeler because, if he responds in the same scientific spirit in which this letter is written, we may prove to be of great help to each other as we grope along these dim corridors.[25]

Following the widely broadcast atrocities of Nazi Germany during World War II, ethics boards were increasingly surveilling and regulating human experimentation. But not all human subjects were treated with the same concern.[26] As one surgeon excitedly remarked, in reflecting on the growing numbers of surgeons who wanted to try out trans surgery, "A patient just wrote to me from the hospital in Chicago where she is undergoing additional plastic surgery. This time, they want to try fashioning the vagina from a part of the intestines."[27] The broader medical community did not vet these experimental procedures.

Within this context of surgical innovation and experimentation in the early 1960s, physicians and endocrinologists were caught in a double bind. They were excited about expanding medical knowledge about bodies and gender, but they also expressed concern that some surgeons might harm trans people through botched surgeries. In response, medical providers began referring patients to each other in the hopes of establishing a base of knowledge and vetting each other to avoid sending their patients to doctors who might harm trans people. The consequences of failed surgical procedures could be devastating to trans people. As scientists, they were trained to think of experimentation as a necessary part of innovation but acknowledged that it sometimes came at the expense of their patients' health and bodily integrity. As Benjamin reflected on one of his patients who sought his help for post-surgical care, "When I think of my patient's terrible experience when someone in Seattle tried to increase the length of her vagina and tore into her rectum, making a permanent rectal fistula, I shudder to think what may happen to other patients."[28]

Experimentation was not exclusive to the surgical realm. Medical providers also experimented with the prescribed levels of hormones administered to trans people. As one trans man wrote to Benjamin in the late 1950s, "I started taking 75 mg orally a day and have increased the dosage to 100 mg a day. What I would like to know is if I increase this dosage to about 150 to 200 mg a day would my body be able to absorb that amount?"[29] Benjamin suggested in his response that he did not believe the trans man should take higher doses, but a definitive answer would require constant observation.

Trans people, too, were worried about the experimental nature of hormone therapies, especially at the hands of inexperienced providers. As one trans woman wrote to Benjamin,

> My doctor has no knowledge in this area and has failed to take any steps to find out. I have consulted several other doctors. I was met with moral lectures and biblical preachings, and disgust. My friend and I need to know what hormones we should be taking, what quantities, what frequency and what determines this. I am enclosing the prescription that we have been on. We were taking the shots once a week and the pills as directed. We have stopped taking the shots as we are afraid we are taking too much. I am off of everything at the present.[30]

As more trans people sought gender-affirming healthcare, providers worked to establish their credibility to the broader profession. But they could not avoid the experimental nature of these medical interventions. To shore up their concerns and avert questions about their morality and medical expertise, providers began turning their attention to the character of trans people. By instituting the trope of the "trickster" trans person, providers deflected professional critiques by focusing attention on the moral character of trans people. This recasting of attention also augmented medical authority to define the boundaries around the set of patients who should be allowed to access medical interventions.

The Trope of the Trans "Trickster"

With no scientific instruments to verify someone as trans, medical providers were keen to ensure that people seeking gender-affirming medical interventions were not lying about being trans and would not come to regret their decision to medically transition. Thus began the development of what I refer to as the caricature of the trans "trickster" in the medical imagery over the course of the 20th century. Providers offered numerous accounts in their personal correspondence with each other of trans people deliberately misrepresenting information about themselves in order to gain access to hormones and surgery. As one provider stated matter-of-factly, "Most of these transsexual patients lie without conscience."[31] This trope of trans people as tricksters—or deceivers, as philosopher Talia Mae Bettcher describes—meant that trans people had to prove their reliability to providers.[32]

Some trans people were aware of the trickster trope circulating in the medical community and sought to assure providers that they were not engaging in deceit. Rather, they asserted that continuing to live their lives in their birth assigned gender was the ultimate deception. As one trans person wrote to the Johns Hopkins Gender Identity Clinic in 1972,

> Please understand that I am writing in earnest and with all sincerity. This letter is no trick and all I write is the truth and not made up. I want you to understand that my need to have this operation is not in passing, but is something of the deepest importance to me and has been for a long time. I can't remember a time when I didn't feel that I belonged to the female rather than male sex.[33]

Like many popular narratives that distinguish between heroes and villains,[34] providers in the middle of the 20th century devoted a considerable amount of energy defining the moral character of their trans patients. Those trans people who felt they could not be truthful for fear that they would be denied access to medical interventions were placed in a double bind in the increasingly rigid expectations that providers placed upon them to acquiesce to medical authority. Noncompliance translated to a definite denial of care, while compliance still subjected a trans person to denial of care if their lived experiences and ways of understanding their gender did not align with providers' expectations. These expectations from the medical establishment outlined a typical trajectory for trans identification. Beginning in childhood, trans people were expected to feel disgust with their bodies, particularly their genitals, and always to want to dress in the clothing and play with the toys of the "opposite" gender.[35] Any deviation from this narrative was met with suspicion by those in the medical community that the patient before them was truly trans.

Trans people were the subject of medical providers' and scientists' curious fascination. As one doctor in the early 1960s remarked,

> This young man who comes from a somewhat substantial family in this part of the country, has assured me that his parents are aware of what he has in mind and are willing to help him financially do whatever he wishes. He has been seen by me some eight or ten times. I have seen him primarily because I was interested in seeing how much breast development a male could accomplish with large doses of estrogen, and other than observe and talk to him, have done nothing.[36]

As this provider made clear, trans people were asked to subject themselves to the scrutiny of the medical and scientific community. The rewards that were used to cultivate acquiescence to batteries of tests and examinations were the possibility of accessing hormones, and sometimes a referral for surgery.

In this era of establishing a base of medical knowledge for working with a growing patient population, providers were also hesitant to work with trans people who had families and children. They began requiring proof that trans people had fully disclosed their desires for surgery to spouses and parents. As Benjamin wrote to a trans person who had sought his help and shared that she had left her family, "I think you made the right decision in leaving your children with their mother."[37] Some providers also ridiculed patients whom they perceived as not being truthful about having families. Below is an extensive quote from a surgeon corresponding about a patient whom Benjamin had referred to the surgeon. The patient had withheld her desires for surgery from her wife and health insurance company, which led to the surgeon cancelling her surgery.

> When [patient name] first came to see me he told me that he was unmarried. A little later he asked me to write his insurance company to ask what part of his hospital and surgical expenses they would pay. They wrote me a surprised letter stating that this man was married and his history didn't seem to correspond with what they knew about him, and that he even had one child. Confronted with this information, [patient] told me that he hadn't told me about the wife and child because he was afraid it would prevent me from doing his operation, which it certainly would. Naturally, I cancelled my arrangements for surgery and told this boy I wouldn't have anything more to do with him from a surgical standpoint, that if he had deceived me in these important points, I felt that he would go on doing so and whose revelation proves his unreliability.[38]

Benjamin wrote in response, "I am not surprised, having had similar experiences before. They simply illustrate the immaturity of many of these people, but I fully agree with you not to have anything further to do with such utterly unreliable girls." The surgeon concluded that not disclosing information warranted a denial of surgery. From his perspective, the trans person was tricking her family and the surgeon and therefore was not a good candidate.[39]

Many trans people who sought the help of Benjamin and his colleagues wrote about how they wanted to disclose their identities to family members but were afraid of being excommunicated. This was a well-supported concern, as many trans people were shunned by their families and publicly humiliated. As one trans person wrote to a provider in the late 1960s, seeking affirmation and pleading for help,

> I am writing to you with hopes that you can help me, because I need it very badly. This is not an ordinary problem that can be discussed with

just anyone, it must be someone who understands the kind of hell I'm going through. I couldn't take being laughed at, and ridiculed. It happened
to me once before, and by a family doctor, no less. I wrote to him, just like
I'm writing to you as a last resort. He did not even have the decency to
reply. He just betrayed my confidence in him and told my family in such
a way, that's too humiliating to think about. This letter is a cry for help,
and I'm begging you to help me please.[40]

More often than not, trans people were encouraged by the medical community to leave their jobs, families, and hometowns to start life anew
where no one knew of their past.[41] As Benjamin counseled one trans
woman, "You will have to stand on your own two feet, and make your
way in the new world that you have chosen. You must consider that a
closed chapter. You are a woman now. Forget all the people that knew
you as a man."[42] This burden of a fresh start also situated trans people
within a lose-lose situation that amplified providers' specter of the cun-
ning trickster. It required trans people to lie—either to their families by
leaving them without explanation, or to themselves and leave behind
the idea of transitioning. For many trans people, this was an unten-
able situation. But the message from the medical community remained
clear: trans people must tell providers everything about their lives and
be exemplary citizens to have the possibility of accessing medical care
for transition-related services. Those who could not meet these expectations were subject to the regulatory power and surveillance of the
medical community and would be denied access to care. This dynamic
was not unique to trans medicine in the middle of the 20th century; it
reflected the predominant model for medical decision-making that has
been described as paternalistic medicine.[43] All patients during this time
were expected to acquiesce to a medical provider's directives. For trans
people, this relational dynamic was fraught with the additional layer of
possibly being outed to family, friends, and community members and
accepting the pathologization of transsexualism through the trope of
the trickster.

Questioning the Credibility of Trans People

In their letters of correspondence with each other, providers shared frustration about the structural conditions under which they were working in trans-specific care. In response, these providers began placing increasing expectations onto trans people to prove that they were trans and, therefore, were credible patients. Embodying traditional gender displays (feminine trans women or masculine trans men) was an ultimate criterion for credibility. But the use of medical authority to promote gender norms and characterize patients as credible aligned with how providers worked with other patients in the mid-20th century. For example, anthropologist Lauren Fordyce documented how, beginning in the 1950s, the medicalization of pregnancy translated to the medical establishment's expectation that women would submit to extensive medical surveillance and advice—over exercise, diets, bathing rituals, avoiding activities that would disrupt peace of mind, and sexual intercourse—to ensure the health of the fetus. These cumulative activities around maternal behavior were tied to gender norms surrounding the hyperfeminine woman. It was assumed that mothers should do everything possible to ensure the health of the fetus, and medical surveillance was a means to achieve that goal. Women were blamed for poor fetal outcomes. A woman's nonconformity to feminine gender norms was a common explanation used by the medical establishment for fetal death.[44]

Providers of trans medicine were also concerned with ensuring that their patients' surgical and hormonal interventions would lead to more gender conformity. Providers questioned the usefulness of enabling gender-affirming interventions for those whose appearance was deemed too masculine for trans women, or too feminine for trans men. As one provider reflected on the goal of surgery for a trans woman,

The outcome of such operations should be viewed from producing a reasonably successful "woman." In this respect, the physical structure and appearance of the patient is of importance. If this appearance is unchangeably masculine, the outcome is, of course, not only problematic, but definitely doubtful if not unfavorable.[45]

In measuring surgical success as helping someone achieve greater gender conformity, medical providers used subjective determinations in their decision-making processes. Trans people, out of fear of being denied assistance, were pressured to conform to these gender-normative expectations and to convince providers they would be able to move through social life in their target gender.[46]

How might an individual move through social life as another gender without the use of physical interventions? This was a question that providers glossed over, as it became established as a baseline criterion for determining whether or not to work with a trans person. If a person could not prove to a provider that they would be able to pass in social life, then what was the point of working with them? In requiring trans people to be gender conforming, the medical community could uphold itself as benevolent and paternalistic for offering aid to "these poor creatures," while relieving themselves of the scrutiny of broader society.[47] After all, they were simply helping trans people to lead normal lives and avoid public attention. As one surgeon shared in his remarks to Benjamin about a trans man who came to him for reconstructive chest surgery,

I have before me the problem of [patient name]. This patient is a mannish, swaggering, deep voiced, somewhat hippy female who at first glance looks every inch a man. Inquiry reveals the fact that there are four or five inches lacking in one area and quite a little too much in others. This patient would like, first, to have the somewhat ample breasts amputated so he can swim with less embarrassment. All of his feminine features are a great source of embarrassment to him. And well they should be, because he is bald and looks so mannish that even one of the very critical doctors [of working with trans people] in our office was taken aback.[48]

For this surgeon, not operating on this "mannish" trans person who was assigned female at birth and had breasts would be unfortunate, as—in his estimation—the surgeon could not fathom any other course of action other than to surgically intervene.

The trope of the trickster was often used to discredit trans people. But sometimes, providers were fascinated by trans people who could trick others into thinking they were a gender different from that assigned at birth. Creating these borders around reveling in trans people who could pass in social life—even without the aid of medicine—as another gender and those who were liars was fraught with bias and frequently reliant upon subjective determinations such as physical attractiveness. As another provider remarked,

> I recently saw a very beautiful woman who came in here. She fooled me completely. She had a man with her with whom she had been living for the last 6 years, and I thought he was going to be the patient. To my great surprise, this beautiful and strikingly handsome woman *was* the patient.[49]

Trans patients deemed unattractive were likely to be denied access to care. "Attractiveness" was a proxy for gender conformity. As another surgeon stated matter-of-factly in his observations of a trans person referred to him for surgery, "My present reason for not wishing to carry out this procedure is that this is a very masculine fellow. My present feeling is that I would almost match him in insanity if I did this job for him. I can imagine that hardly a jury in the world would condone it."[50] As this surgeon observed, the appearance of the trans person mattered greatly in making the decision to withhold surgery, alongside a subtle suggestion that the patient was mentally unstable for assuming that she could pass in social life as a woman. Unconvinced, the surgeon denied the patient access to surgical interventions.

Tied into appearance-based concerns, the demeanor of patients was also a criterion for providers' litmus test as to whether or not they would proceed with medical interventions. As one doctor wrote to a patient requesting information on how to find a surgeon, "Good luck. I hope you find the help you desire. Certainly if you are as lovely as your picture, you should have no problem."[51] Trans people not only had to convince providers that they could move through social life in their target gender by following gender-based appearance norms, they also had to uphold normative gender roles. As one surgeon congratulated Benjamin for a referral with whom he was pleased,

> We are very grateful to you for your kindness in sending [patient's name] to us. The patient stated that her present job is a nurse aid at a local hospital. She came in dressed beautifully in feminine clothes and altogether appeared to be a very nice young lady—quite nice looking. She said that she had been under your care for a year and that during this time she has passed as a female this entire time without once being questioned or even being stared at.[52]

Trans patients who narrated identities closely aligned with traditional gender ideologies regarding women's and men's roles in society were readily granted access to hormone therapy and surgical interventions. For example, medical providers were suspicious of trans women who worked in male-dominated professions such as construction. They expected that following a gender transition, trans people would shift into more "suitable" and gender-normative work. As one doctor observed, in assessing a patient's readiness for surgery, "Patient lives alone and works as a clerical worker at a local steel plant. He has held this job for five years. At the end of our meetings, the patient planned to go into nursing after his sex reassignment. During high school he worked as a nurse's aide and he enjoyed this work."[53] This doctor eventually concluded that the patient was a homosexual transvestite with strong transsexual leanings but needed to experience living in social life for one year as a female before he would perform any surgical interventions. Within this context, providers simultaneously counseled trans people who worked with children, such as teachers, to find different occupations, as they might be fired from their jobs if discovered to be trans. Providers and surgeons counseled each other to deny access to care or turn away trans patients who refused to follow these recommendations.[54]

Into the 1960s, more providers began to mandate that their patients live for a year in their target gender. Referred to as the "real life test"— where a trans person was expected to live their life as if they had already physically transitioned but without the aid of hormones or surgeries— the milestone of one year in one's target gender was used by providers to determine if trans people were committed to "going all the way" in accessing surgical interventions.[55] Yet contained within the naming of this test is the tacit idea that trans people's lives, up until the moment that they sought medical care, were not real. Providers denigrated trans people, in their letters of correspondence to each other, for having unrealistic ideas, goals, and expectations for the outcomes of trans medical interventions. To help validate their credibility in claiming a trans identity, putting a hold on trans-specific interventions enabled providers to test their patients' commitment.

Furthermore, in creating this test, medical providers could also assure themselves that their patients were not making a rash decision. They counseled patients writing for help that surgical interventions were a serious undertaking. As Benjamin wrote to one such patient, "Your desire to have your sex changed requires very serious consideration. Before such an operation, which is an irrevocable step, can be advised, a very thorough examination and several months of observation under hormone treatment would be necessary, as well as a consultation with a psychiatrist."[56] And the patient wrote back, "You called my desire for a sex change operation an irrevocable act, which it is, but it is not something I just decided to do yesterday. I've thought about it a long time. I want to be a woman."[57] One year later, the same patient wrote to Benjamin again asking for help. She shared that changing her sex had become a "grand obsession" for half of her adult life, and that she was finding it more difficult to live with her "masculine role."[58] Benjamin's curt response indicated his doubts that this person was a credible candidate for surgery, "It would be advantageous to discuss your problem with Dr. P. who is a very understanding psychologist. He could then report to me which would be helpful for my advice for you in the future. I believe Dr. P. could make it easier for you to live in your 'masculine' role."[59] In his opinion, this person was not a credible patient and the best course of action was for the patient to learn to live in her assigned sex.

In creating implicit rules for trans people to follow before they would be allowed access to trans medical interventions, medical providers established a way of thinking about trans patients where those who were deemed unable to pass in social life as their target gender were not credible. Thus, the idea of the credible trans person was also built upon the mandate for trans individuals to maintain normative gender expression and demeanor and could move undetected through social life.[60] For trans women, this meant being preoccupied with makeup and maintaining hyperfeminine appearances, settling down, finding a husband, and tending house. For trans men, the expectations were to find stable jobs and support one's wife.[61] Yet providers were doubtful that most of the people who came through their clinics and asked for trans-specific medicine could assimilate into social life as their target gender without raising the attention of those around them. Indeed, drawing any public attention to one's self was met with a swift denial of care from the medical community. As Benjamin counseled one patient who swore she had no interest in public attention on herself, "Publicity must, under all circumstances, be avoided."[62] So thoroughly entrenched was the concern for ensuring their patients would not publicly announce that they were trans, lest they draw international media attention like Christine Jorgensen, providers discredited these patients' stated desire to have trans-specific medical interventions, and sometimes also their humanity: "I believe, of course, these people are picked on but, my gosh, they certainly are a screwy lot having such an obsessive yen for publicity."[63]

Establishing Worthy Patients

Examining the etymology of "normal," disability studies scholar Lennard Davis found that with the emergence of scientific discourse and statistics that sought to quantify and measure everything against an average, bodies became standardized too.[64] This process of standardization helped create notions of average bodies, where those falling outside the norm were understood as deviant. Furthermore, as disability scholar Rosemarie Garland-Thomson has asserted, making such distinctions within medical communities translates to what bodies should look like and what they are expected to do.[65] Individuals, or bodies, that fail to uphold such expectations are marked as "other" and treated in kind by the medical and scientific community as a problem to fix. For example, scholars studying the medical establishment's treatment of intersex infants have found that it is informed by the assumption that having an ambiguous sex is a problem that should be solved by surgical intervention to create a normal appearance.[66] In the process of making distinctions between normal and abnormal, the medical establishment accrues more regulatory power to define what is normal.

What makes medical understandings of normal bodies so difficult to break down or change is that through the power and authority of science, normal/abnormal distinctions become canonized in scientific thought and further used to uphold providers' claims to expertise.[67] The medical establishment began to take for granted the idea that trans people were not normal but, through medical interventions, could be transformed into normal people. As one young scientist wrote to Benjamin in the late 1960s,

I am encouraged to take the next step and compare groups of transsexuals and normals by their EEG. I know I can bring to this analysis a more sophisticated approach. Then, if all goes well and shows each transsexual to be different from normals, I think this will be something surgeons and others will have to accept and it will significantly improve the situation.[68]

As this scientist articulated to Benjamin in explaining his research design, trans people were juxtaposed against the classification of normals, which placed them as being perceived by the medical and scientific community as abnormal. Defined within a double standard, few trans people could pass the high expectations that providers placed upon them to demonstrate their normalcy. As a result, medical providers established normative ways of life for trans people. The best course of action—from the perspective of the medical and scientific community—was to attempt to normalize trans people's bodies and lives as much as possible.

These broader social lenses for scientific and medical community concerns related to abnormality help us understand why medical providers were so wary to work with trans people who had families, in that they might corrupt otherwise "normal" people—especially their children. As Benjamin wrote to an attorney who was working with a trans patient on a custody issue, "I thought it would be better for her children's future not to grow up with a father who lives as a woman. I thought she should not oppose the adoption and should be willing to make a sacrifice, as long as she wants to continue her present form of living."[69] One concerned wife wrote to Benjamin asking for help to make sense of her trans spouse. This individual shared that she supported her spouse's decision, and that they had a healthy relationship, but she wanted clarification on how her spouse might access trans-specific surgical interventions. Benjamin responded, "Any radical steps like surgical sex change should not even be considered. The good will on the part of both you and your mutual respect for each other could eventually reduce the problem to less and less importance."[70] The sacrifice of one's family became a litmus test for medical providers to see how far their trans patients were willing to go to access medical interventions. And if a family was relatively stable and "normal," according to the perspective of medical providers, why bother disrupting the home life so that a trans person may medically transition?

Concerns with normalcy were so far reaching that trans patients who exemplified any abnormal behaviors or flaws were sometimes regarded as nonhuman. One provider shared the following story with a surgeon about a patient:

> This patient was arrested after using the lavatory for females in a restaurant of very questionable reputation. She was taken to jail and booked for vagrancy. . . . The patient came in to see me, giving me a long cock and bull story about the nature of her arrest, little of which I believed, and the next day one of my more faithful transsexuals came in with a close account of all that had happened because this patient had been present on the night of the arrest. My [faithful] patient stated that the patient arrested had recognized someone clear across the room and called out, "Yoo hoo! I'm a woman now; I have been operated on by a surgeon. Yoo hoo!" Then she used the toilet and got arrested. This man is now out on probation and expects me to write a letter to the Deputy City Attorney of the Criminal division to keep him off the hook. . . . I just mention these things to you to keep you from being troubled further by this creature who is carrying one of your letters.[71]

Trans people who were arrested on charges of vagrancy for using restrooms or dressing in clothing not aligned with their sex assignment at birth were subject to the additional surveillance of law enforcement. The letter that the provider quoted above refers to was perceived as a way to help some trans patients avoid legal action taken against them if they were discovered by the police to be "masquerading" as a gender different from the one assigned at birth. This provider further suggested that the trans person was not deserving of such a letter because she publicly proclaimed to have had gender affirmation surgery. Thus, in his estimation, the provider denounced this trans person and concluded that she was not deserving of protection from the law.

Trans people faced increasing scrutiny from the medical community to become model citizens with no hint of moral imperfection. Having a criminal record, a history of using drugs, or any indication of being socially "undesirable" subjected a trans person to the scorn of medical providers and denial of care. As one doctor pondered, "Should we punish the 'good and deserving' transvestites because some others behave so abominably? After all, that's part of their illness. They're irresponsible misfits."[72] These social "misfits," as some providers were wont to refer to their trans patients, were treated in contradictory ways. Providers assumed their patients aspired to lead "normal" lives, through the aid of medical interventions, but still regarded trans people with great suspicion and as exotic "others." White trans people who held steady employment were perceived as the most suitable candidates for physical interventions.[73] These criteria that were used to determine worthy candidates for medical interventions were further shaped by classism. As reflected in a note from Benjamin to a doctor who had referred a trans woman to his New York practice,

> [Patient name], of whom you wrote to me, finally came in to see me. He had hitch-hiked to New York and arrived penniless. Typical of these immature 'he-shes' isn't it? I examined him and confirmed your diagnosis of transsexualism. I advised him to hitchhike home to his mother in Colorado. Heaven knows what he will do.[74]

In this instance, Benjamin confirmed for the doctor that the patient was trans. But rather than offering medical services, he sent the person away. Infantilizing the trans person by suggesting that he told this person to "hitchhike home to his mother," Benjamin deemed this person unworthy of his medical expertise because she could not fulfill the implicit requirement of being a productive citizen. By infantilizing this trans woman, Benjamin justified his paternalism while upholding his medical authority to deny access to care.

Indicative of the wide-reaching classism that seeped into healthcare clinics and encounters, even the administrative assistants to medical providers who were sought out by trans people regarded working-class trans people as unworthy. Take for example the following correspondence from a patient to a physician:

Dear Dr. [Name],

I want to have the sex change operation from male to female. I want to know how much this will cost and how long. I have very little money and I want this done free, and if you know of a doctor who will do this free, let me know. I want to meet you, let me know when you are coming to LA. I would like to have this done here or in your office. Also, I need a home and money and employment. Do you know of anyone I can stay with?[75]

The doctor's administrative assistant responded to this request by suggesting,

Dear [Patient name],

Let me explain to you that the doctor is not a surgeon. He never operates. The so-called "sex change" operation that you are interested in is a very serious undertaking and would require hospitalization for at least three weeks. Before any such operation could be advised a long and careful study of the patient would have to be done, and there are no surgeons in the United States at present who would even then undertake the operation. The doctor thinks it would be best for you to take your family physician into confidence and follow whatever advice he may have for you.[76]

Many trans people who did not come from middle- or upper-class backgrounds were unable to access trans-specific care. What limited information we have in the historical record indicates that trans people, such as the patient from the correspondence above, were dismissed outright and scolded by the medical community. Providers were hesitant to see trans people who had tenuous finances. As one remarked to a patient who asked if there was any financial help available for surgical interventions, "Our patients mostly work and earn and save the money themselves."[77]

For trans people seeking medical assistance, they also had to contend with mid-20th century discourses of "doctor knows best" where patient challenges to medical authority were not met with the same reception as they may be today, in a time of patient consumerism and the loosening of providers' authority in medical decision-making. By establishing a base of medical knowledge that was largely built upon gender norms, culturally situated assumptions related to identities were entwined with moral imperatives of worthiness and subsequently became canonized as scientific fact. Yet these moral imperatives that were applied to assessing trans people's worthiness hinged on broader cultural discourses. "Worth" was used by the medical community to uphold ableist notions of the productive citizen. As one patient reflected in a letter to Benjamin,

> My life, to say the least, has been frustrating, confusing, and unhappy because the way I feel, the future I want, the things I need, desire, and want from life are not "normal" and therefore wrong. But all of these things are so natural and right to me. I don't believe that I'm terrible or wicked or insane yet I know I have problems that need working out. I sincerely believe that I have goodness in me and something positive and constructive to give.[78]

As this trans individual suggested in her reflection, she acknowledged that some people in broader society might not perceive her trans identity as normal, but she insisted that it felt right for her. To assert her request for medical interventions, she further shared that she was neither wicked nor insane, but that regardless, she had something that she could give back to society. Poltical scientist Dan Irving's research on the medical community's treatment of trans people has demonstrated the importance of economic factors related to productivity.[79] An additional element of patient worthiness can be found in the entanglements of classism, ableism, and upholding normative gender presentations.

Medical providers directly linked notions of being productive citizens to perceptions of a patient's worth. In one letter, Benjamin reflected on a patient who he doubted could blend into social life:

[Patient] is somewhat paranoiac character, and a low IQ doesn't help matters. It may be the best, at least for the time being, for "her" to revert back to a masculine status, masquerading so to say, as a man, and take a man's job as in former days. Of course, there will be no new surgical procedure.[80]

Commenting on her IQ, Benjamin drew from already-circulating ideas used in the feeble-minded campaigns, which sought out social undesirables including the poor, people of color, and sexually active women to label them as unworthy citizens, and then forcibly sterilized those deemed unworthy to prevent from reproducing.[81] Ideas of unworthiness and intelligence were tied to the medical community's investment in social fitness. Sometimes subtly, Benjamin and his colleagues used a purity framework to understand their trans patients, too. As one medical provider remarked in a letter to another provider, "Should we allow them to have children? You suggest that we leave the testes in place. But performing this as a part of it [genital surgery] is paramount." In the scramble to find surgeons and physicians to extend the networks of providers who were willing to work with trans people, they reached out to the Association for Voluntary Sterilization for recommendations for other providers.[82] In the absence of surgeons willing to work with trans people, providers assumed that trans people's desires for medical interventions might be best handled by surgeons already familiar with sterilization procedures.

Providers believed that a "successful" trans person was one who left their family and had surgery that removed any possibility for reproduction, and they coached trans people to concede that they may never again be involved in sexual or romantic relationships—and certainly not ones that might produce children. Thus, trans people in the 1950s and into the 1960s were regarded by the medical and scientific community alongside other populations of people—including black women and men,[83] poor people,[84] and sexually active women[85]—as undesirable others.

These medical understandings of difference had a longer lineage rooted in eugenics and shaped by social discourses around social fitness. Trans medicine was not immune to these trends, as the development of sexology and endocrinology in the early 1900s was shaped not only by advancements in gender differentiation based on expression (e.g. masculinity and femininity) but by the advancement of "The Race," which was defined in regards to white, respectable, and affluent people.[86] Providers of trans medicine working in the mid-20th century joined a historical legacy of using scientific knowledge and medical interventions in the name of dealing with so-called "deviant" bodies.[87] As sociologist Henry Rubin details, endocrinologists working in the 1930s used synthetic hormones to "cure" sexual inverts, later termed homosexuals.[88] At first the scientific community thought that homosexuals had a deficiency in testosterone. When treatment failed to correct homosexual behavior, endocrinologists turned to using estrogen to render homosexuals sexually inactive. Scientific understandings of how hormones work, and to what effect, were applied to many other groups of people who were "deviant," including criminals, intersex people, and people of color.[89] Mid-20th-century providers of trans medicine followed these trends and used medical interventions on trans people's bodies to help bring order to perceived social disorder in the changing definition of gender.

2

Legitimacy Wars between Physicians and Therapists

At a loss for how to determine which patients who requested gender-affirming care should receive it, physicians in the 1960s began leaning on a small group of psychiatrists and psychologists for help assessing trans people's requests to begin hormone therapy and surgical interventions. Rather than working together in a team approach, these communities erupted in professional disputes as each healthcare arena advocated for their way of understanding trans people and the appropriate steps their patients should take toward a gender transition. As I will show, these epistemic clashes involved disagreements over who should have the power and legitimacy to claim trans medicine under professional jurisdiction. They clashed on a basic question of whether or not medical interventions were warranted for trans people. The small group of physicians who had been working with trans people since the 1950s thought it best to eventually allow medical treatment, as they had direct observations of how much hormone therapy and surgery helped improve the lives of trans people. Therapists, however, recommended extensive therapy for trans people and believed that medical interventions were, for the most part, inadvisable—especially without patients first being vetted by a therapist.[1] As the mental health community was increasingly called upon to help evaluate trans people, epistemic clashes also emerged between psychiatrists and psychologists. They presented a united front to physicians. But there was no consensus among them on how to define transsexualism, how to assess a patient's claims to this identity, or which branch of mental healthcare was best suited for trans medicine.

This chapter details the messy and complicated pathways by which medical professionals traversed an emergent area of medicine permeated by uncertainty and lack of consensus in definitions, treatment protocols, and assessing patient groups. In the scramble to assert and retain power, physicians engaged in intense legitimacy wars with mental health providers in a power grab over trans medicine. The clashes between psychiatrists and psychologists reflected broader skirmishes between mental health communities in the US. In the 1960s and 1970s, psychiatrists faced broad criticism for using invasive and experimental treatments. Meanwhile, psychologists were becoming empowered as the public supported less invasive treatments such as talk therapy.[2] To regain a foothold, psychiatrists leaned on their medical training and held themselves up as scientists, advocating for diagnostic categories and standardized treatment protocols. By the early 1970s, perhaps out of necessity, psychiatrists and psychologists eventually began to create agreed-on protocols for working with trans people. Anything less, and they might have lost their relevancy in trans medicine if they couldn't present consensus opinion on how best to work with trans people.

The Erosion of Power among Physicians

Just a decade into their experimental procedures in hormone therapy and surgical interventions, physicians of trans medicine in the 1960s began to acknowledge that they needed better tools to identify truly trans people from those whom they perceived as delusional for seeking gender-affirming interventions. They had already begun to create criteria for weeding out unworthy patients and those who were understood as "transvestites," which was clinically defined as people who desired to dress in the clothing of the "opposite" sex but harbored no disgust with their genitals or other sex characteristics.[3] But physicians were increasingly aware that they needed the mental health community for guidance on assessing trans people who had mental health problems or for verifying those patients they were suspicious about claiming to be trans. During this time, physicians assumed that most trans people were "extremely unhappy, on the verge of suicide, and ungrateful" for not recognizing the effort that physicians went through to help them obtain gender-affirming care.[4] In light of these concerns, the handful of physicians working with trans people remained convinced that medical interventions were the most effective means for helping trans people. It may have been with ambivalence that physicians invited therapists into the work of trans medicine. But with their introduction, physicians witnessed their own power chipped away.

Of great concern for physicians was the expanding jurisdiction that psychiatrists and psychologists began to assert in trans medicine. Soon after their invitation to work with physicians in evaluating trans patients, they also began making recommendations for allowing or denying access to gender-affirming care. Physicians thought this was an overstep on the part of the mental health community. They perceived the proper role of therapists to only be involved in evaluating trans patients' mental health. In response, they began to voice criticism of their mental health colleagues and question their legitimacy. Firm in their belief that medical interventions were the only way to help trans patients, Benjamin and his colleagues questioned if therapy had *any* value in the lives of trans people. As Benjamin wrote to a doctor, "I finally received copies of the psychological tests. I think they are quite useless."[5]

Given their lack of appreciation for therapy in being able to alleviate suffering among trans people, physicians were particularly critical of those who advocated for long-term therapy as a necessary part of a gender transition. As Benjamin shared with a colleague, "Yes, I was shocked when I heard that [name of psychologist] wanted the patients to have 6 months of psychotherapy, and that in spite of the fact that Freud did not feel that sexual deviates could be helped by psychoanalysis."[6] While it was initially conceived by physicians as a one-time visit to a therapist, mental health workers balked at this expectation. Instead, they began asking their patients to establish extensive therapeutic relationships.

To further question the legitimacy of therapists, physicians also took them to task for creating financial burdens for trans patients seeking surgical interventions. Physicians were especially prickly about the power the mental health community was increasingly being granted from surgeons. As one physician wrote in a patient report to Benjamin,

> I had a fine-looking handsome woman who came in with a man with whom she had been living with for six years as a husband. . . . She said she had about $1,400 (saved for surgery) and wondered if she could perhaps get started on her operation. Believe it or not, the surgeon said that she ought to have $7000. He said he wants her to go to a couple of lawyers and he wants her to go to a couple of psychiatrists. Like you, that makes me very angry, because one glance at this beautiful woman and you know that she should be a woman, and she should always be allowed to dress as a woman and live as a woman. There is no need for examining her at great length. The surgeon wants both a psychologist and a psychiatrist to work with her.[7]

Previously surgeons would ask that the referring physician work with a trans patient for several months on hormone therapy, recurring appointments, and then write a letter on behalf of the patient ahead of surgery. With the introduction of mental health into the transition process, surgeons began requesting that a psychologist and psychiatrist independently evaluate the surgical candidate. Benjamin cautioned his physician colleagues that "the examinations by a psychiatrist and a psychologist may be a protection [for the surgeon], but for the patient they are an added financial burden and—to my mind—often unnecessary if not misleading."[8]

Ultimately, physicians were caught in a double bind of their own making: they wanted the mental health community to validate their recommendations for trans patients seeking surgery, but they found themselves losing exclusive claims to authority in trans medicine.

Epistemic Clashes among Mental Health Professionals

As mental health professionals were invited into trans medicine and began trying to make sense of transsexualism, epistemic wars between psychologists and psychiatrists erupted. The nature of these professional disagreements reflected broader trends in US mental health communities during the middle of the 20th century. Medical sociologist Owen Whooley has documented how this time period was a pivotal moment for the mental health community in trying to establish themselves as experts.[9] Psychiatrists working in the 1960s and 1970s faced multiple affronts to their authority. First, psychiatrists were not a homogenous group. Some aligned with Freud's psychoanalytic theories and took detailed patient histories to determine what elements from a person's background might cause mental disturbances;[10] others drew on biomedical theories, which were complemented by the rise of psychopharmacology around the 1960s to treat mental disorders.[11] Second, there was also an active antipsychiatry movement that vocalized opposition to crude and scientifically unsubstantiated treatments such as lobotomies and shock treatments.

During this time, psychologists were beginning to carve out their own professional jurisdictions and vied for power with psychiatrists. They found public support for less invasive treatments such as behavioral and talk therapy. In response to the growing power of psychologists, psychiatrists sought to restore legitimacy to their profession through the establishment of standardized diagnostic categories that appeared in the *Diagnostic and Statistical Manual of Mental Disorders* (DSM).[12] Before the late 1970s, classification was not as important to the practice of therapy, and diagnostic categories had little bearing on the everyday practices of those in the mental healthcare community.[13]

Physicians took advantage of the internal bickering that had emerged among psychologists and psychiatrists and became more vocal about casting suspicion on the psychoanalysis favored by some psychiatrists while belittling the value of behavioral therapy that was popular among psychologists. Creating a fissure between psychologists and psychiatrists enabled physicians to retain some authority over trans medicine as those in the mental health community fought about how to best proceed in trans medicine. As Benjamin reflected to a medical provider, "It seems ridiculous to me that my patient should not be able to have the psychological tests done by most anybody in the field of psychology. They are not supposed to make recommendations but merely list the test results. The principal medical report comes from the psychiatrist."[14]

Biomedical psychiatrists responded favorably to physicians recognizing their legitimacy in establishing protocols in trans medicine. They attacked psychologists for naïvely assuming that therapy alone would cure trans people. As one psychiatrist quipped, "If one thinks of psychotherapy for the transsexual in terms of changing or 'curing' them, then you're just barking up the wrong tree. It isn't going to happen. And the great majority of them [trans people] simply have no motivation to try to affect any change."[15] As this psychiatrist suggested, it was the moral failings of trans people that explained the inability of psychological intervention to cure them of their gender problems.

Biomedical psychiatrists attempted to elevate their power by asserting that their work was scientifically rigorous. They also pointed to how their branch of mental health was a leader in diagnostic criteria that would standardize the assessment of transsexualism. But rather than merely accepting psychiatrists as primarily responsible for diagnosing and treating transsexualism, psychologists shot back by questioning how these classifications were defined, and for what purpose. For example, in the mid-1960s, transsexualism was understood as a type of schizophrenia by psychiatrists, but as hysteria by psychologists.[16] The following case notes from a meeting of mental health professionals debating the underlying cause of transsexualism demonstrates the conflict in definitions and diagnostic processes:

DR. D: Patient is alcoholic, gets in trouble—ends in hospital, often her own cry for help. Same pattern repeating over and over.

DR. G. said, "Erratic, delusional, hallucinatory." Although he considers
patient psychotic, such people can make satisfactory relationships
and could be treated.

DR D.: Conclusion, "Ambulatory schizophrenia"

DR. G. What will be—is—our definition of schizophrenia?

DR. M. wondered if it always schizophrenia in transsexual patients

DR. G: Very much in need of help, very disturbed, in need of
psychotherapy.[17]

As the meeting proceeded, a psychologist remarked, "It seems to me
to be more berserk behavior, hysterical psychosis, not schizophrenia."[18]
To name transsexualism as a form of hysterical psychosis made sense
from the perspective of mid-20th-century psychologists. The definition
of "hysterical psychosis" included behaviors that occurred suddenly and
dramatically with "manifestations in the form of delusions as likely dis-
tortions of reality which disappear when emotional control is achieved
through psychotherapy."[19] In this rendering, transsexualism could simply be alleviated by extensive therapy, with no need for gender-affirming
surgical or hormonal interventions.

With the deinstitutionalization movement underway by the 1960s
and the growth of the healthcare insurance industry, psychologists were
awkwardly aware that housing patients in long-term treatment facilities was no longer feasible or desirable, as the public was concerned
about the burden of such facilities on taxpayers.[20] As they fought with
psychiatrists about the proper diagnostic classification, psychologists
had to contend with their professional desire to work with patients
over an extended period of time with shifting public opinion and fewer
government-sponsored resources for inpatient care. Thus, being able to
hold a job and remain independent from the state became a formal part
of psychologist's assessment protocols in whether or not to recommend
a patient for surgery.

The mental health community may have been uncertain about what
caused transsexualism, or what diagnostic category to place it under.

But one thing was clear for those working in mid-20th-century mental health services: identifying as trans was a symptom of delusional thinking, and anyone who wanted to "change their sex" was met with suspicion and labeled as having some form of psychosis.[21] The diagnosis of transsexualism as a deviant category created a stigmatized lens through which the mental health community understood their patients. How to treat transsexualism, however, remained an open dispute.

Creating Professional Legitimacy

To elevate their legitimacy and professional standing, therapists borrowed from the strategies that physicians had used over the 1950s and into the 1960s. This included using similar stances as physicians in assessing the appearance and intelligence of trans people to determine viable candidates for surgery. But therapists had their own spin on what criteria trans people needed to meet to be deemed eligible for gender-affirming care. They had a particular fascination with the sex lives of trans people. Those engaging in normative sexual practices were approved of by therapists. Trans patients engaging in so-called deviant sexual behavior were frowned upon, as they were assumed to be homosexuals masquerading as trans people, seeking gender transitions to avoid the stigma of homosexuality prevalent during the middle of the 20th century. Therapists, especially psychiatrists, began using the language of science to buffer themselves from critiques by the public and physicians. Psychiatrists and psychologists sought to establish their knowledge about trans people as legitimate, as each wanted to take lead in this new area of mental healthcare.

Invoking the Perspectives of Physicians

Like their physician counterparts, therapists mandated conformity to gender norms, as it was assumed that the only reason a trans person should undergo medical interventions was to be able to move through social life undetected as trans.[22] They often used the appearance of trans people, pre-transition, to assess how well a person might fare after hormone therapy and surgery.

Appearance was taken so much for granted in the patient intake process that therapists rarely offered explanations for how appearance mattered in making their psychological assessments. For example, as one psychologist who had extensive mental health training and was a leader in the field remarked in a letter to the referring doctor, "Patient has always thought of himself as a woman and there is no question in my mind that he is a transsexual. He plucks his facial hair and wants electrolysis. I have no doubt that he is a true transsexual and could well begin hormones now."[23] As this psychologist observed, the patient before him created no doubt that she was truly transsexual as she performed proper femininity. Voicing approval for this patient, he was particularly taken with how well this patient kept up her appearances and conformed to beauty standards. What made her distinct from other patients who may have been denied access to care was that she carefully curated her facial hair and electrolysis was a planned step in her gender transition to help further feminize her appearance to outside observers.[24]

Dichotomous ways of thinking were not unusual for the mental health community, as they were trained during an era when people were classified as either mentally ill or healthy with no fine gradations in between. Like their assumptions about people either being ill or healthy, therapists tended to characterize trans people in dichotomizing ways—as passive or aggressive, beautiful or grotesque, stylish and feminine or frumpy and masculine. As one psychiatrist wrote about his first impressions of a trans patient referred to him by Harry Benjamin,

> The patient arrived at the appointed time, neatly attired in a black dress, dark cloth coat and calf-length boots which were appropriately stylish. Her hair was neatly and rather sophisticatedly styled. It was difficult for the examiner to note any frankly masculine qualities in either this patient's bearing or demeanor. Her overall cooperativeness

ensure that the test results would be a valid and reliable indication of her present functional level.[25]

Historians have documented how "passing" was an ultimate criterion for mid-20th-century trans people to access medical interventions.[26] But therapists were concerned with more aspects of a trans person's life than whether or not they could pass in social life as their target gender. The patient mentioned above was approved of by the psychiatrist because of her appearance and how she presented as appropriately feminine and stylish, too. She received additional kudos because of her demeanor, which amplified the perception that she was truly trans. Lacking any frank masculine qualities, this patient surpassed gender-normative expectations and became someone who, from their assessment, had a high likelihood of employability through her punctuality and neat attire. In contrast, unemployment and not appearing appropriately gendered was a red flag for providers. These life attributes were used against trans people to question their character and their commitment to trans identification. For example, in one trans support group meeting, a psychologist facilitating the meeting noted that "[patient name] projected complete negativism, contributing nothing, is unemployed, and was the least feminine of all who attended."[27]

Therapists, like physicians, were also concerned with matters related to intelligence. As one psychiatrist wrote to a surgeon in the late 1960s,

Psychiatric evaluation of [patient name] revealed an intelligent, cooperative, pleasant, obese, manly-appearing female. At this time, the patient seems to be in general touch with reality, oriented to time, place and person. The contemplated gender change was thoroughly discussed, and emphasis was placed upon the irreversibility of the procedures she desired. I see no psychiatric evidence at this time that would contraindicate the indicated procedures.[28]

Written in clear prose, this psychiatrist established as scientific fact how IQ, mannerisms, and gender conformity created no doubt in his mind that the trans person should have access to surgery. Cooperation with the medical community was viewed favorably, as was a pleasant demeanor. Scoring low on intelligence assessments brought almost immediate denial of care from the medical establishment. But therapists were also concerned that a highly intelligent patient seeking a gender transition might have too much wherewithal and trick them into believing that they were trans. Thus, we can also see in the case notes and letters of correspondence that therapists borrowed the trope of the trans trickster, as discussed earlier, from their physician colleagues in how they evaluated trans patients.

For therapists, the trickster was linked to their professional field-building activities in sorting through and refining classifications for sexual and gender minorities. In spite of the diagnostic ambivalence that psychiatrists and psychologists had regarding whether or not transsexualism was a type of schizophrenia or hysteria, some therapists believed that trans people were really homosexuals.[29] They were apprehensive about high-functioning and highly intelligent patients who identified as trans and wondered if they might be seeking gender-affirming interventions to avoid the stigma of being labeled homosexuals in broader society. As one psychologist wrote in a report summarizing their general impressions of a patient who was referred for assessment,

> Patient appears to be a stable intelligent young man with nothing to indicate serious psychological disturbance. He does have strong transsexual leanings, however, he has made an unusually good adjustment as a male homosexual with some transvestite features. During the time of this evaluation, patient has made no plans or gestures to live more completely as a female.[30]

The psychologist signed off on the patient's ability to obtain hormones but expressed doubts in the patient report about this course of action.

From his perspective, the patient had already made a good adjustment as a homosexual who might feel fulfilled enough by cross-dressing, rather than going through the process of a gender transition.

The intelligence levels of trans people helped mental healthcare providers feel assured that trans patients could be productive and capable citizens. As one psychologist remarked,

> Although patient appeared to be depressed it was my impression that this was on a situational basis and I saw no evidence of either endogenous depression or schizophrenic reaction. The patient is of normal or above normal intelligence and shows no evidence of mental illness. I believe she is capable of making valid decisions as to her own life.[31]

Not having a mental illness became a crucial distinction for whether or not a trans person should begin interventions. As such, therapists also felt justified in asserting their authority to comment on matters related to social fitness, which was defined as being able to acclimate to normal life. In appropriating the perspectives that physicians used to determine worthy candidates, therapists augmented their professional authority. But they needed additional ways to distinguish their skill set from physicians. To do this, they turned to a subject firmly in their domain: taking explicit sexual histories.

Detailing the Sex Lives of Trans People

The family was often a site of regulation for trans people's sexuality and civic productiveness. As discussed earlier, trans people who wanted to keep their familial ties intact were often denied gender-affirming care. The medical establishment was resolute that trans people needed to break free of their families and children. Like physicians, therapists emphasized in their patient assessments how trans people should leave their families and children and only engage in heterosexual relationships upon transitioning (trans women should partner with cisgender men and trans men should partner with cisgender women). From their perspective and reflected in their referral letters to each other, "changing sex" enabled people to be in heterosexual relationships. As one provider stated,

> Although some female hormones (preferably at a low level of intensity) might be helpful now to reduce his anxiety, I feel that any further move toward TS should be done very cautiously. His motivation for change may well be linked to his desire to be accepted by his last lover as a female.[32]

The written correspondence of therapists was fraught with contradictions. On one hand, they wanted to ensure that people were not seeking gender-affirming medical interventions to avoid their homosexual desires. On the other hand, providers determined that the only permissible relationship option was for trans patients seeking partners that would be identified as heterosexual by outside observers upon transitioning.

What defined these relationships as normal was established by the kind of sex that one had prior to surgical intervention, and what kind of sex a trans person desired to have after transitioning. As one doctor in the mid-1970s wrote in a widely circulated brochure for medical providers who had questions about working with trans people,

> This (having a sexual relationship) is a simpler matter for the male-to-female transsexual because her anatomy after surgery lends itself to the more usual modes of intercourse. But she may be concerned about children in marriage, and here I can assure her that if she and her husband meet the usual requirements of adoption agencies, it will be possible for her to have a family just like any other woman. Now the female-to-male transsexual, even if he has had a phalloplasty, will have some special concern, in addition to not be able to impregnate a partner. As you know, to date, the constructed penis does not function for sexual intercourse.[33]

Heteronormative by default, therapists assumed that trans people would eventually want to establish a family upon transitioning. In their imaginings, a trans woman would cater to the needs of her assumed cisgender male partner and penetrative intercourse was the optimal goal. Furthermore, therapists assumed that trans women would seek opportunities to fulfill this destiny by adopting children, as their motherly tendencies would become apparent upon transitioning. In contrast, therapists were concerned that trans men may have more difficulties in heterosexual relationships, as these providers were quite phallocentric and assumed that trans men could never fulfill their duties in being a "real" man by engaging in penetrative intercourse. Thus, as the provider above reflects, trans men presented an affront to the expectations of heterosexuality, as they could not impregnate a partner. For both trans men and women, penetrative heterosexual intercourse was assumed by the medical establishment as a way to achieve normality.

Owing to the legacy of psychoanalysts such as Sigmund Freud, mid-20th-century psychiatrists were emphatic about detailing their patients' histories and, in particular, their sex lives. They added to this aspect of the evaluation process a fascination with the sexual proclivities of their trans patients and flagged anything that did not conform to heterosexual penetrative intercourse. Using a case report approach, many in the mental healthcare community took detailed notes on the sexual practices and desires of their trans patients. This manner of scrutinizing the sexual practices and desires of patients is unsurprising. As other scholars have noted, beginning in the 17th century, the mental health community has had much to say about the "perversions" of masturbation and homosexuality and other sexual practices that are deemed non-normative.[34] In staking their authority on distinguishing between normal versus deviant sexual behavior, therapists assumed it was well within their wheelhouse to comment on the sexual practices of their patients. It was also widely accepted that those who failed to conform to social standards were mentally ill.

The consequences of therapists weighing in on normal versus deviant sexual practices extended beyond the classification process of diagnosing mental illness. In a detailed analysis of this history, Ladelle McWhorter suggests that therapists used these so-called perversions to uphold racial domination through scientific racism, by describing certain sexual practices as "animalistic," "uncivilized," and "spoiling the blood lines."[35] In this scientific rendering, masturbation weakened and corrupted the purity of white people, as it was emblematic of having a weak will. This way of understanding masturbation was not relegated to the 1800s. In the middle of the 20th century, psychologists were still concerned with people who masturbated. And trans people were not exempt from the moralizing of masturbation by the mental health community. Not only was it perceived as "perverse," masturbation was used by the mental health community to disqualify a trans person from accessing medical interventions. As one psychiatrist said in a published interview intended to help outreach and education efforts to a broader audience of therapists outside the close circle of those specializing in trans healthcare,

> One of the most important indicators I look for in taking a sexual history is masturbation. In the transvestite you usually get average or high rates of masturbation. But for the transsexual, the rate is usually very low. . . . And of course, if you get a male with an extensive history of heterosexual relations, you must question whether he is a transsexual. This is another sort of contradiction you will be on the lookout for.[36]

Masturbation became an implicit indicator in mid-20th-century classification systems for transsexualism. High rates of masturbation were understood as indicative of transvestism because to do so was assumed to mean that a person was not disgusted by their genitals and found pleasure in having sex. In contrast, trans people were expected to never masturbate because if they hated their genitals so much that they wanted to alter them through surgical interventions, they would never derive pleasure from them.

Using Scientific Language

During the 1960s and into the 1970s, therapists increasingly turned to using the language and methods of science to increase their legitimacy in trans medicine. Psychiatrists perceived that the most effective way to retain a foothold was to align themselves with physicians by asserting their training in medicine. This strategy fit within the broader project of medicine during this era, as the profession—with the exception of psychologists, who were leaning more toward behavioral interventions—became increasingly grounded in biomedical models of illness.[37]

While physicians had already expended great effort sorting through differences between homosexuals and trans people, and between trans people and cross-dressers, the mental health community's immersion into trans medicine brought renewed interest in discovering the etiology, or origins, of transsexualism. They were absorbed with identifying symptoms and constructing a diagnosis to help explain people and behaviors that fell outside of the norm.[38] In naming transsexualism as a mental health disorder, therapists assumed responsibility for identifying psychological flags that would suggest whether or not a patient was someone who suffered from mental illness or was truly trans. As one psychologist wrote about a patient,

> This 20-year-old, never-married transvestite comes from a very disruptive background. . . . I feel that he is essentially a masochist, fetishistic transvestite. He is obsessed with his looks, is desperately trying to look more like a female. He has already had a rhinoplasty. He refuses psychotherapy but is certainly in badly in need of it. He is in no way a transsexual, although he does want female hormones and wants his face to look like a female's.[39]

In the mid-1960s, "transvestites" were ineligible for gender-affirming interventions because they were defined by the medical establishment as people who simply cross-dressed and therefore were not in need of gender-affirming care.[40] On the basis of this distinction between transvestites and transsexuals, the psychologist in the above correspondence assumed hormones were unnecessary for this patient, while gesturing toward the patient's mental instability for seeking hormones in the first place. The psychologist concluded that while the patient may want to look more like a female, in his determination the patient was certainly not trans.

In a very short amount of time, therapists shifted their stance from pondering the origins of transsexualism to reifying diagnostic codes for the purpose of identifying "true" transsexuals. Conducting research was a key driver for establishing a scientific basis in therapeutic interventions for trans people. It was during the middle of the 1960s, after all, that trans medicine shifted from being practiced exclusively in private clinics to newly opened gender identity clinics associated with prestigious universities.[41] This set the stage for research feasibility, as more subjects availed themselves of these clinics in the hopes of obtaining medical interventions. As one psychoanalyst detailed in a letter to Harry Benjamin about new developments in a research project,

> I am writing in respect to my role in our research project on transsexualism. These interviews and diagnostic testing will concentrate on the direct elicitation of pathological and attitudinal expressions. Consideration will be given to anxiety, depression, reality distortions, regression, and other experiential phenomena. Effort to understand certain aspects of etiology as well as diagnosis on a personality level will be made. Psychopathological evaluation and prognosis are to be emphasized.[42]

By the early 1970s, the psychiatric community had come to some agreement that transsexualism was a distinct category from psychosis and neurosis. In one exemplar of a letter written to Harry Benjamin from a psychiatrist who was asked to assess a trans person, we read,

> Patient is a 35-year-old white divorced genetic female who I saw for seven visits with the final diagnosis of transsexual. The patient has had a psy-

chological male orientation since childhood. The preferred sexual object has always been female. Attempts with male sexual objects have been fraught with frustration and failure. It is my opinion that this genetic female would be benefited by bilateral simple mastectomies and male hormone therapy on a continuing basis. I do not find this patient to be suffering from any psychosis or significant neuroses.[43]

How this psychiatrist articulates the patient's history and diagnosis of transsexual is in a direct manner that conveys authority of the subject matter. While earlier therapeutic evaluations were prone to more ambivalence and less matter-of-fact evaluations, by the 1970s, therapists spoke with the authority of experts that classified and diagnosed trans patients using the language of science. In so doing, they alleviated themselves of some of the scrutiny of their fellow colleagues who were beginning to question a therapist's role in working with trans people.[44] Some therapists believed that it was quackery to work with trans patients in any manner other than treating them as delusional.

Constructing a diagnostic category for transsexualism helped psychiatrists gain legitimacy and buffer themselves from critique by other psychiatrists. But they faced the dilemma of not having much data to support their work. In response, therapists relied on using the language of scientific evidence in a way that philosopher Ian Hacking has referred to as classificatory looping, where the categories that are created offer a certain way of thinking about people who might fit within a diagnosis. Stated differently, evidence that fits a diagnosis is upheld as evidence of the existence of the diagnosis, which further legitimates the diagnostic category.[45] The mental health community could preserve their importance in trans medicine by making their diagnostic categories and assessment procedures a necessary part of gender-affirming care.

Through classificatory looping, therapists also standardized ways of thinking about and treating trans people. As another psychiatrist wrote matter-of-factly to a trans patient,

You manipulate people in an unconscious fashion as a part of an over-all type of manipulativeness that we have come to recognize as part and parcel of the personalities of many individuals with gender disorders. Let me say candidly that at this point in time you are not deemed, for your own best interests, a good candidate for immediate sex conversion, and we cannot give you a definite date in the future other than to say you are on a hold status.[46]

The psychiatrist upheld his authority and maintained control over the patient by refusing to write the requisite letter of referral to begin medical interventions. This psychiatrist leveraged anecdotal observations to speculate about the typical trans person who suffers from manipulativeness and therefore was untrustworthy.

"Treatment" was not exclusive to trans-specific therapy. Therapists had before them the task of offering therapeutic services outside of the gender identity component of trans medicine. Toggling between trans-specific mental health assessments and more generalized mental health evaluations proved to be a challenging task, as therapists often conflated the two. As one psychologist reflected,

Subject is a 45-year-old married transvestite. He is unemployed and has a very poor work history. He has been a transvestite since a very early age. He wants to become more feminine and would even like hormones and an operation. He has been in mental hospitals and has had electric shock. I feel that this person can only maintain himself on a very marginal level and that really not very much can be done for him from a psychological standpoint.[47]

The patient described in this letter presented the trifecta of problematic patients from the perspective of therapists. Like physicians described earlier, therapists also used classist, ableist, and gender norms to withhold treatment from anyone that provoked suspicion about claiming to be trans. With her "poor" work history, the psychologist doubted that she could financially support herself or pay for the services for medical interventions. Yet lurking in the background of this letter of correspondence is also the notion of productive citizenship. If a person cannot hold a job before transitioning, how could they possibly function after such a drastic life change? Further complicating this person's history was that she had received electroconvulsive therapy and had been previously admitted to inpatient mental health facilities. Given the wide-reaching stigma toward people with mental illnesses, this mental healthcare provider cast away the patient and assumed that nothing could really be done for her within trans medicine or broader therapeutic treatments.

Into the 1970s, psychiatrists and psychologists eventually came to consensus that trans people were deeply disturbed and established gatekeeping practices to keep—from their perception—unstable people from obtaining medical interventions. They engaged in classificatory looping by building up a classification system to identify "truly" trans people. These classifications were aided by the deployment of scientific language that further established the authority of therapists in trans medicine.

Creating a Place at the Table

By the mid-1970s, trans people were increasingly regarded by the medical establishment as a group of people who required the services of *both* mental and physical health providers. Together they imposed rigid standards on trans people and outlined "ideal" cases—or those patients who were determined worthy of obtaining medical interventions, raised no suspicion about being trans, and could prove that they would be model citizens. Providers began emphasizing a routine patient intake and assessment process.[48] They required extensive and ongoing psychological evaluation, as well as the "real life test." Trans people were also expected to present in public spheres at all times as their target gender. Anything less was treated with suspicion by the medical community that the patient was not willing or ready to go all the way. From their thinking, a prolonged test drive in a different gender would help offer, as one provider suggested in a published interview, "the best index of judgment for eliminating non-transsexuals [from consideration for surgical interventions]."[49]

These protocols became dispersed across the small, but growing, network of providers in the United States who were working in trans medicine. As one director of a counseling center told an interested human service worker about the process for working with trans people in the late 1970s,

> At least two of us on the team interview each person laying claim to be a transsexual and then our psychometrician tests them. Further, we require that they have at least 2 years of psychotherapy, with one of those years lived, dressed and worked in the gender of their choice. It is only after the patients has gone through our minimum requirements that they may then request of us that we recommend them for surgery. At that time, they are fully tested again, and we have a conference to determine if this is a suitable candidate for that purpose. If we approve an operation, we then furnish the patient with the most up to date list we are able to acquire of all the ethical, competent surgeons presently in the field, from which they may choose the physician of their choice.[50]

The language with which the director described the protocols highlights how trans medicine was well on its way in accumulating a body of knowledge from which medical providers drew to help each other learn the emergent norms in the field, the assumptions made about trans people, and consensus in protocols.

In these professional field-building activities, however, trans people were boxed into a lose-lose situation as their agency in the process of gender-affirming care was disregarded by the medical establishment.[51] Confronted with the limited option of either accepting the medical community's labels of "sick, bad, and perverted" or refusing to acquiesce, trans people faced incredible barriers to accessing trans-specific care. As one case file detailed,

> At a hospital where the patient was sent after his disappointment over failure to achieve surgery, the hospital reported that the individual is completely conditioned and no form of psychotherapy or any other medical approach can convince this individual that he must assume to role of a male and live out his life as one of masculine character. One of the problems in this type of case is the operation should not be performed. The patient should be hospitalized for one year for psychotherapy. Hospitalization would remove the socio-economic stress and place the patient in a position of dependence which would make psychotherapy more feasible.[52]

The medical establishment infantilized trans people who would not assent to the growing demands placed on them. The golden age of doctoring, where medical authority reigned, was already declining by the late 1960s. But medical providers were accustomed to treating marginalized groups differently and assumed that for those deemed abnormal, medical authority should be asserted to help bring order to perceived social disorder.[53] Cast as benevolent in using medicine for charitable acts, the psychological community was increasingly called on to psychologically classify normal from abnormal persons. Trans people fit within the medical establishment's schema of abnormality, which enabled physicians and therapists to form consensus and begin working together.

Identifying Ideal Cases in a Team-Based Approach

Using a team approach helped physical and mental healthcare communities share resources and build a more united front against growing criticism from colleagues and probing from the press. During one team meeting in 1966, for example, a few providers from Johns Hopkins shared that they had recently received unwelcomed national press attention for the work of its Gender Identity Committee (GIC). Providers affiliated with the GIC wanted their activities to remain outside the purview of public comment, as it helped them continue their work without the scrutiny of colleagues in other areas of medicine. Being out of the public's eye also inhibited potential patients from seeking access to their services. As they noted, more people were reaching out to the GIC and the staff were overwhelmed. In response, the committee wanted to resolve the issue of "how to decide upon an ideal patient. Certain clearcut types should be avoided, i.e. psychotic and those with serious legal difficulties."[54] Linking their concerns to needing to ensure that trans people were not "delusional and hallucinatory" or "psychotic,"[55] therapists and physicians needed each other to maintain their legitimacy to the broader medical community.

Using the authority of scientific discourse to quell critiques of the experimental nature of the work they were doing also helped reaffirm the mental health diagnosis of gender identity disorder while addressing physicians' stated concerns to identify strong candidates for medical interventions. As one GIC case file reflected,

Childhood conditioning questionable; patient always "hoyden"[56] and tomboy. 21-year-old brother was sissified. Father hoped for boy at patient's birth. No pregnancies or abortions. Makes very good impression dressed as male. No contraindications for surgery. Patient deeply desires such surgery and should be able to function quite satisfactorily on social, economic, and other levels. Such surgery is recommended.[57]

In this case file, the patient passed the standard tests that the medical community had established. Placing the origins of transsexualism in childhood rearing confirmed the theory that mental illness stemmed from one's childhood background. Presenting as appropriately masculine and being able to support one's self financially and move through social life undetected as a trans person were all check boxes asserted by the psychiatric and medical community that added up to a golden ticket for this patient to receive the go-ahead for surgical interventions.

The ability for physicians and therapists to work together was aided by the fact that these communities had already been borrowing ideas from each other on what indicators to look for in trans patients seeking medical interventions. Consider the notes from another case file of the GIC that represents how each community of health professionals wanted to see evidence of trans people being productive citizens after transitioning:

> Childhood conditioning questionable; patient was raised as a boy, but father encouraged and requested patient to do housecleaning, ironing, washing, and cooking. Psychological impression—feminine habitus. No history of venereal disease. Does not drink, smoke, or use drugs. Patient urgently requests such surgery and should be able to function satisfactorily on all levels as a woman.[58]

Trans individuals who may have come from a challenging childhood environment were somewhat suspect. But not engaging in risky or illegal behavior, and therefore avoiding legal troubles, was understood by the medical community as a stronger indicator that a patient could function as a normal person upon transitioning.

There was also growing consensus across physicians and therapists that trans people needed to leave their families. A successful transition was defined when a trans person could start new romantic relationships:

> Patient was seen by the doctor together with wife and a couple of children and dressed as a female. Strongly discouraged by the doctor. Patient at initial exam was very tense and nervous, although dressing nearly every day. Patient urgently requests operation and it is felt she could make a good adjustment as a female. Has been living and working as a female since 1965. Has offer of marriage from male after surgery.[59]

As early as the 1950s, as I previously suggested, physicians had begun to establish a protocol for trans people to leave their children and spouses before transitioning. With the team approach, this expectation was supported by consensus among providers. From their perspective, a trans person who stayed in their relationships might be perceived by others as homosexuals (e.g., a trans woman staying with her wife in a romantic relationship). From this committee report, it was advised that the trans patient should accept the marriage proposal, even though her spouse supported her transition.

As therapists and physicians continued to work together, the legitimacy wars began to ebb. As a result, they began to augment each other's professional authority and claims to expertise. But not all trans patients were amenable to going through the process prescribed by these medical communities, with extensive therapy recommended first before beginning hormone therapy or surgery. As one patient shot back to Benjamin, who had asked her to see a psychiatrist first before he would see the patient for a physical and write a recommendation for surgery,

> I don't by all means need to visit a psychiatrist to get an ok from him or her, whoever it may be because after all, I'm a grown man and at the age of 38 and don't need to have anyone's consent to undergo an operation like the one I have in mind. I hope you don't think I'm being harsh about my feelings, for I am very calm and patient as a person can be.[60]

Asserting the need for a psychiatric evaluation, Benjamin's administrative assistant responded, "It is Dr. Benjamin's rule to have a psychiatrist recommend the operation if such is at all possible. When you meet Dr. Benjamin, he can refer you for a psychiatric evaluation."[61] As this administrative assistant made clear, therapy became a tool not only to evaluate a trans person's mental fitness, but also to dissuade some patients from seeking gender-affirming medicine.

Just as physicians were ambivalent about what role therapists might play in the transitioning process, mental health professionals also had ambivalence about whether or not trans people could be helped by therapeutic interventions alone. Over time as the legitimacy wars between physicians and therapists—and between psychiatrists and psychologists—subsided, medical professionals agreed that their role was not to cure trans people. Rather, it was to ensure first and foremost that people who sought trans medicine were not delusional, homosexuals, or transvestites. Together, they also agreed that trans people should be gender conforming, free from familial constraints, passive and model citizens to be considered worthy of medical interventions.

The expectation that became solidified by the end of the 1970s was that trans people's access to gender-affirming care was best addressed by both physicians and therapists. As the 1970s came to a close, trans medical providers had new concerns to confront together. With the end of paternalistic medicine, and broader shifts in medical knowledge and training that began emphasizing patient-centered care and evidence-based medicine, they had to respond to the problem of evidence in trans medicine. Into the 1980s, therapists continued to refine the diagnosis of transsexualism and psychologically assess trans people. Physicians were in charge of trans people's hormone therapy and frequent physical examinations. As a united front, they began to create clinical guidelines and standards of care for working with trans people. But, as I will show, in trying to standardize treatment, these mid-20th-century legitimacy wars cropped up again in trans medicine as disagreements about the classification of transsexualism and treatment protocols continued to be a point of contention among healthcare professionals working in trans medicine.

PART II

Contemporary Trans Medicine

3

Making It Up

Evidence in Contemporary Trans Medicine

In the opening remarks to the morning plenary during the 2013 National Transgender Health Summit, the past president of the World Professional Association for Transgender Healthcare (WPATH), Eli Coleman, enthusiastically described how a working group of "leading experts in the field of transgender medicine" had crafted revised standards of care (SOC).[1] To bring trans-affirming medicine to a global level, the new SOC were dispersed through alliances across continents and translated into 23 different languages, a notable feat that Coleman shared with the excited audience of over 300 medical practitioners, community organizers, and trans people. Coleman lauded the WPATH as an organization that previously was complicit in pathologizing individuals, but now had evidence-based medicine at the center of its mission. Continuing to explain some of the key features of this new version of care, Coleman suggested that "an important revision was the inclusion of scientific evidence in the new standards, where previously there was none."

Coleman's comments mirror a prevalent contemporary narrative regarding how trans medicine in the United States has shifted over the 20th century. Many providers I observed at trans-specific health conferences, and spoke with in interviews, were quick to claim that things have gotten better for people seeking access to gender-affirming healthcare since the early days of trans medicine. Trans patients, contemporary providers suggest, no longer experience such extreme stigma by the medical community as they did in the middle of the 20th century. Providers point to the establishment of professional documents such as guidelines and diagnostic criteria as proof of improvement over time.

These documents are part and parcel of the evidence-based medicine (EBM) movement that emerged in the 1980s in response to critiques from the public that medicine needed to become more objective, standardized, and less biased through greater use of scientific evidence.[2]

The march toward accumulating scientific evidence has included many areas of contemporary social life, among them the medical community.[3] In seeking a stronger scientific base in medicine, EBM symbolizes a growing datafication in medical decision-making.[4] At its base, EBM is informed by systematic review and analysis of existing literature to help construct best practices.[5] The discussion of scientific evidence that appears in protocols, standards of care, and diagnostic tools is ranked according to the reliability and verifiability of research. Randomized control trials are at the top of this hierarchy, and providers' reports and case studies are at the bottom.[6] Trans medicine has not been immune to these data-driven changes, and considerable resources have gone into establishing stronger claims to scientific evidence, aided by the construction of clinical guidelines and diagnostic criteria. Many medical providers herald EBM and the creation of more refined formal documents as a solution to problems that plagued trans medicine in the past. Paradoxically, in looking beneath the surface of these documents for trans medicine, the evidence that is cited often does not meet the medical establishment's definition for valid scientific evidence.

This chapter explores how contemporary providers construct evidence to bolster the legitimacy of trans medicine by codifying agreed-upon norms surrounding gender and outlining a "proper" gender transition. I begin by examining the assumptions that shape formal documents, including the diagnostic criteria and clinical guidelines in trans medicine. I analyze these documents as symbolic artifacts that increase the professional power of providers by offering a rhetorical tool to draw from to align trans medicine with trends occurring across the medical establishment.[7] After examining these formal documents, I then turn to informal ways in which providers construct evidence. More difficult to discern because of the implicit manner in which it shapes decision-making, the informal evidence that providers draw on—accumulating clinical experience and gut instinct—helps them parse through conceptions of risk while amplifying their authority.

Constructing Evidence through Diagnostic Codes

Currently, trans medicine is diffused across areas of specialization and continues to rely on both physical and mental health interventions. In physical healthcare, family care physicians, gynecologists, and endocrinologists work with trans people in everyday medical encounters and provide trans-specific healthcare such as estrogen or testosterone hormone therapy. In mental healthcare, counselors, psychologists, and psychiatrists work with trans people through everyday concerns as well as transitioning-related therapy. Some trans people seek medical interventions, such as hormone therapy or surgery; others interact with the medical community by way of mental health providers. These pathways to care are rooted in mid-20th-century understandings of who should treat trans people, and in what kind of "disordered" object is implied with treatment. Is the goal of treatment to bring the mind into alignment with the body, or to change one's body to bring relief to one's mental health state?[8] The answer to this query has never been fully resolved in trans medicine, as physicians and therapists continue to disagree with each other about who should have authority to decide when a person may begin medical interventions or what circumstances should prevent a person from obtaining gender-affirming care. As a result of these ongoing disputes, the medical establishment has concentrated on refining the diagnostic code for what is now called "gender dysphoria" and outlining the appropriate sequence of steps a person should follow before being granted access to gender-affirming care.

Today, each time a healthcare provider sees a patient, they must code the reason for the visit and any medical intervention that is prescribed for both record-keeping and insurance purposes. An exhaustive list of insurance companies that covers or denies trans coverage is difficult to find. Coverage varies widely across insurance companies and the stake-holders they work with.[9] Blue Cross Blue Shield, for example, does not exclusively ban trans coverage. But in working with the state of North Carolina, which voted to remove trans coverage from state policies beginning in 2018, the insurance company was obliged to follow the desires of the state.[10] No insurance company can cover treatments, however, without a diagnostic code to process the expense.

Diagnostic codes serve a utility function (e.g., insurance reimbursement). They are also cultural artifacts symbolic of the medical community's sense-making of disease and illness categories.[11] What comes to be recognized, and then labeled as a disease, is socially negotiated and reveals the values of medical stakeholders.[12] Like other diagnostic categories, gender dysphoria "locates the parameters of normality and abnormality, demarcates professional and institutional boundaries of social control and treatment, and authorizes medicine to label and deal with people on behalf of society at large."[13] For example, as historian Jennifer Terry (1999) has described, without clear boundaries around which to define their work, therapists went to great efforts to classify homosexuality as a pathological problem and codified it as such in the first two versions of the *Diagnostic and Statistical Manual of Mental Disorders*, a virtual "bible" for psychiatric illnesses.[14] Even after its removal from the *DSM-III* in the 1980s, gay activists were suspicious that the sudden appearance of a new diagnostic category called "gender identity disorder" was a guise for a continued understanding of homosexuality as a medical problem that could be cured by psychiatric intervention.[15] The results of these efforts by the psychiatric community have been well documented in the existing literature, as gay people were sometimes exposed to what we would now consider brutal treatments from the mental health community. Curing homosexuality entailed physical, psychological, and emotional abuse.[16] From the medical establishment's perspective, gender conformity or a lack thereof served as a proxy for "normal" people compared to homosexuals. Efforts to regulate gender nonconformity through diagnostic codes have continued, although implicitly, in trans medicine.

The process of creating a diagnostic category, or changing the definition of one, is not seamless. Many disputes occur in what we can think of as these category-creating activities in the medical profession. Well documented in the existing literature, the diagnostic category for "gender dysphoria" is a double-edged sword; having a diagnostic category offers some promise that insurance companies will reimburse the expenses paid out of pocket for gender-affirming interventions, but the existence of a diagnosis suggests that being trans is an illness.[17] The diagnostic category is also in dispute among those within the medical community.[18] As we saw in the previous chapter, therapists debated whether claiming a trans identity was a manifestation of delusional thinking and, therefore, a type of schizophrenia. This idea no longer holds much weight among therapists, yet it is one example of the complicated ways the medical community has relentlessly tried to codify nonnormative expressions and behaviors into a coherent and diagnosable category.

Simply naming something as real lends credence to its realness, as sociologist Anne Figert demonstrated using the case of PMS to show how diagnostic categories represent consensus-based knowledge by medical communities. PMS is contested as an illness, with disagreement on whether it is a natural part of the menstruation cycle or indicative of an underlying mental or physical health issue.[19] Other examples abound in the history of medicine where the construction of diagnoses creates a medical problem of a life event to ensure medical control over people's bodies. The diagnosis of hysteria in the mid-19th century offered a medically sanctioned mechanism for surveilling people's bodies and regulating women who acted in gender-nonconforming ways.[20] Nonetheless, many providers continue to work from the assumption that diagnoses are anchored in science and therefore devoid of social values regarding proper bodily expression or behaviors.[21]

Without bioindicators, the existence of novel illnesses is questioned by the medical establishment. Instead, providers might regard a patient's physical symptoms as evidence of an underlying mental illness.[22] Lyme disease is a contemporary example of how the medical community initially dismissed the realness of the disease because they were unable to biologically test for it. Most of what was known about Lyme disease came from patients' self-reports, and providers failed to recognize and treat Lyme disease for quite some time.[23]

In contrast to the development of the diagnosis for Lyme disease, in trans medicine the medical establishment moved quickly to classify transsexualism. This process was enmeshed in providers' fragile expertise. Providers in the mid-20th century publicly presented as experts, but their private correspondence with each other shows their own misgivings on what their role should be in working with trans people. As more mental health providers began working with trans people, accumulating medical knowledge further solidified the assumptions they brought into this medical domain. Today, medical and scientific knowledge has slowly shifted to relying on biologically essentialist notions of gender and sex: while a person can change their gender through physical alterations, their "true" sex remains what a person was assigned at birth by doctors.[24] With no biological or psychological tests to definitively determine if someone is trans, the diagnosis remains disputed.

The two major organizations currently involved in creating diagnostic manuals include the World Health Organization (WHO), with its *International Classification of Diseases* (*ICD*), and the American Psychiatric Association (APA), with its *Diagnostic and Statistical Manual of Mental Disorders*, 5th Edition (*DSM-5*). The *ICD* standardizes the diagnostic inventory of diseases for an international medical community. A new version of the *ICD* (version 11) was released in 2018 to much fanfare by trans advocates but will not be formally adopted until January 2022. In version 10 of the *ICD*, "transsexualism" was one of several subcodes within a broader diagnostic category of "gender identity disorder." Transsexualism was previously defined as

> Severe gender dysphoria, coupled with a persistent desire for the physical characteristics and social roles that connote the opposite biological sex.

The urge to belong to the opposite sex that may include surgical procedures to modify the sex organs in order to appear as the opposite sex.[25]

This definition of transsexualism alludes to the 1950s-era trope of the
trickster, wherein trans people's bodies are modified to appear as, rather
than become, another sex. While a subtle conveyance, the *ICD-10* has
broader implications in defining real trans people as those individuals
who understand their bodies as simply needing to be changed to fix a
problem. In the *ICD-11*, transsexualism has been renamed to "gender
incongruence" and defined as

A marked and persistent incongruence between an individual's experienced gender and the assigned sex, which often leads to a desire to 'transition', in order to live and be accepted as a person of the experienced
gender, through hormonal treatment, surgery or other health care services to make the individual's body align, as much as desired and to the
extent possible, with the experienced gender. The diagnosis cannot be
assigned prior the onset of puberty. Gender variant behaviour and preferences alone are not a basis for assigning the diagnosis.[26]

In the previous version, the WHO had left little room in the creation
of a diagnostic category for nonbinary or trans people who may seek
medical interventions but do not wish to "cross" over to another binary
gender. In the recent version, the emphasis on incongruence between
experienced gender and assigned sex allows for nonbinary people to
receive transition-related care.

Structurally, gender identity disorder used to be classified in the *ICD*
in the F60 range of codes, or disorders of adult personality and behavior.
Symbolically, this conveyed to the international medical community that
like narcissistic personality disorder (code F60.8) or pedophilia (F65.4),
trans people's identities should be understood as behavior or personality
disorders. Sociologists Georgiann Davis, Jodie Dewey, and Erin Murphy
have suggested that the diagnostic process for gender dysphoria "gives

gender" by naming and explaining proper gender identification within a narrow range of possibilities. As they describe, in the process of giving gender, providers pathologize trans people because of the implicit assumption that they are fixing a gender problem.[27] In the *ICD-11*, gender incongruence was moved out of the index for mental health codes and placed in a new area for "conditions related to sexual health." This change signals that the medical establishment no longer regards being trans as a mental health condition. But, in moving gender incongruence into a classification for a sexual health condition, they have re-conflated gender and sexuality categories.

Maintaining how gender incongruence is a "condition," the medical establishment remains committed to understanding gender incongruence as a medical problem that can be biologically fixed. If the goal of treatment, according to the *ICD-11*, is to "make the individual's body align, as much as desired and to the extent possible, with the experienced gender," then providers retain control over embodied gender. With the ultimate outcome of aligning the body with the mind, physical health providers have formally written jurisdictional authority over gender transitions into the diagnostic process.

Providers sustain a biologically deterministic accounting of gender by defining it as something that resides internally in one's body and is expressed outwardly. Like Eli Coleman, whose story of progress opened this chapter, many believe that thinking about gender in this manner will lessen the stigma associated with being trans because it is something that one cannot psychologically change.[28] Using a "born this way" narrative has been popular among mainstream LGBT communities in the last several decades.[29] LGBT activists have asserted their right to legislative protection as a minority group within this framing. While this is persuasive, social psychological research demonstrates how stigma actually increases when illnesses or behaviors are defined from a biological perspective. Instead of garnering sympathy, using biological determinism to understand an identity leads to the perception that the person is difficult to control.[30] Within the diagnostic process, gender complexity becomes simplified, while augmenting the authority of the medical community.

Like the WHO, the APA has moved away from binary assumptions of gender and has more flexibility built into the diagnostic category. In the most recent diagnostic manual, the *DSM-5*, the APA changed the name from "gender identity disorder" to "gender dysphoria." As they suggest, this change removed the connotation that a trans person was disordered.[31] Gender dysphoria is defined by the APA as an "incongruence between the gender assigned at birth and the experienced/expressed gender, that may include alternative gender identities beyond binary stereotypes."[32] In the *DSM-5*, emphasis is still placed on the primacy of a person's gender identity in defining all aspects of social life, and the assumption that most individuals experience distress because of their trans identity, rather than the social conditions that may create distress for trans people. Prioritizing the difficulties associated with being trans, the medical establishment has also excluded the possibility that being trans may bring joy to one's life. In spite of the advancements in the diagnostic categories and creating more inclusive definitions, gender dysphoria has the distinguishing feature of being the only diagnostic category to appear in the *DSM-5* with no cited evidence to support its diagnosis or prognosis.[33]

The medical community's knowledge of trans people has changed over time and the definitions and symptom lists that are offered in diagnostic categories have become more flexible with each version released. The underlying assumptions contained in the contemporary diagnostic codes are similar to mid-20th-century understandings of trans people as tricksters who desire to pursue medical interventions to change their sex characteristics. The medical establishment's definition of gender dysphoria restricts the ability of trans people to self-advocate for medical interventions beyond the values and norms codified in the diagnosis.

Accruing Legitimacy through Evidence-Based Medicine

Sometimes referred to as "cookbook" medicine, guidelines and standards of care are intended to aid medical decision-making by simplifying the diagnostic process and offering ready-made instructions on how providers should proceed through treatment options and plans.[34] Clinical guidelines represent professional field-building activities in EBM as they are typically supported by scientific research. Unlike a large swath of guidelines for other diagnostic categories, in trans medicine there are no controlled trials on the risks or benefits of medical interventions. It would be difficult to produce randomized clinical trials for gender-affirming interventions because such a small number of people seek trans medicine. However, the guidelines in trans medicine are supported by case studies and patient reports from medical professionals.

Two professional associations have come to dominate the issuance of clinical guidelines. The World Professional Association for Transgender Health (WPATH) is the oldest association that specializes in outlining the provision of trans health and education of the medical and mental health community about recommended care options. The Endocrine Society in recent years has established its own clinical guidelines, as many trans people seek out the services of endocrinologists for hormone therapy. The WPATH guidelines are supported more often by therapists, while the Endocrine Society guidelines are supported more often by physicians.[35] Comparing these guidelines shows the subtle but significant difference in perspective from these epistemic communities and reflects earlier disputes between therapists and physicians during the mid-20th-century legitimacy wars. The tone of these documents conveys authority by using the language of science and EBM.[36]

These documents introduce new providers into consensus-based knowledge of gender-affirming care. Like diagnostic tools, guidelines convey assumptions made by the medical establishment about the appropriate definitions for, and treatment of, trans people. Mandated therapy has been one of the more contentious features of the guidelines as it creates a gatekeeping relationship between trans patients and therapists.[37] But, not all physicians or therapists believe that therapy should be a requirement for trans people and admit that the evidence for this historical practice has been sparse. For example, during a summit on trans health that I observed, Eli Coleman (the former president of WPATH) said,

> We [psychologists] have to humbly acknowledge that we don't have a scrap of evidence that shows therapy is critical. While this was stated in previous versions it is now clearly stated that psychological counseling is not a requirement to access medical intervention. We still maintain *when deemed necessary*, a referral to a specialized health professional is recommended.[38]

Sitting in the audience, I looked around, surprised by this statement, given the efforts of the medical establishment to legitimate the need for psychological evaluations. In just a few sentences, Coleman identified a central point of tension between trans people and medical communities, and therapists and physicians, since the mid-20th century. No one in the audience seemed to react, other than to nod their heads in agreement. What struck me about this particular moment in the conference is that on the one hand, the role of therapists in trans medicine has become an established routine in the decision-making processes of physicians and surgeons in gender-affirming care; on the other hand, Coleman suggested that there is no evidence to support the mandate for therapy, and no evidentiary basis for recommending therapy was ever existent in the first place. At the same moment that Coleman humbly submitted to the audience of medical professionals that there is no evidence to mandate therapy, he qualified his previous sentence by countering that therapy may still be deemed necessary in particular circumstances. This exception muddles WPATH's public stance refuting mandated therapy, as there was no further discussion of what evidence a therapist should use to determine when a referral might be necessary. Seeking a more patient-centered approach to gender-affirming care, WPATH currently recommends a mental health screening for referral for hormone therapy, but psychotherapy is not a requirement. Conducting a health screening may be less stigmatizing, and more affordable, than mandated therapy for several months as the previous guidelines recommended. But the health screening allows therapists to retain authority over trans people's gender transition process.

The Endocrine Society presents its guidelines as more reflective of current practices than the WPATH.[39] In 2017 the Endocrine Society, like the WPATH, conceded that psychotherapy should not be a requirement for adults seeking hormone therapy, and it is now a recommendation. For hormone therapy, adult-aged trans people are now asked to find a clinician who is "competent in using the DSM" and obtain a diagnosis of gender dysphoria/gender incongruence before beginning hormones.[40] Following the therapeutic evaluation and diagnosis, according to the guidelines, the endocrinologist needs to confirm the diagnosis before beginning treatment. In recommending the need to confirm a therapist's diagnosis, the therapist's role in trans medicine is subordinated to endocrinology.

Even for therapists, the psychological assessment for evaluating a trans person's readiness for interventions remains opaque, as the assessments are indeterminate. WPATH has recognized in recent years how therapy cannot "solve" gender dysphoria. In the broader medical establishment, gender conversion therapy has been repudiated and it is now consensus opinion that one cannot be converted from transgender to cisgender.[41] However, because the diagnostic process for gender dysphoria is murky and there are no biological indicators for determining whether or not someone is trans, there remains ambivalence in the guidelines surrounding how to verify gender incongruence. The Endocrine Society has taken advantage of the ambiguity to elevate its authority.

For gender affirmation surgery, the Endocrine Society recommends that surgeons seek the advice of an endocrinologist and a mental health professional, a recommendation for surgery should not be made until at least one year of "consistent and compliant" hormone treatment has been accomplished, and surgeons should not operate until after the endocrinologist has cleared a trans person for surgery. This multi-stage process places a significant burden on trans people to demonstrate their eligibility as surgical candidates. In asking for consistent and compliant hormone treatments, the guidelines convey that worthy patients are those who are passive to medical authority and willing to subject themselves to constant surveillance.

Trans people are in a lose-lose situation in these ongoing jurisdictional disputes over diagnosis and the necessary steps one must take in gender-affirming care. Not following the guidelines might result in denial of interventions. But following the guidelines and directives from the medical community situates patients in a less powerful position. Within the scientific discourse of evidence, patients have little room to claim expertise over their own bodies and gender identities.

While the guidelines help medical professionals accumulate authority through the rhetoric of evidence, they ironically do not have a strong foundation of scientific evidence. To buffer themselves from critique, while acknowledging that there is little evidence, phrases such as "in spite of the lack of evidence, we suggest" or "Evidence is, to date, inconclusive however" populate these formal documents.[42] The professional associations that publish guidelines for trans medicine have followed the broader medical establishment's evidence-grading system. This system has a ranged scale from "very low" to "high quality" ranking for evidence. Caveats are linked to each recommendation, often appearing as a technical comment based on the correct dosing of hormones or monitoring blood labs. Like the WPATH's, the Endocrine Society's guidelines caution that in trans medical interventions, "the evidence comes from the unsystematic observations of the task force and their preferences." The thin scientific evidence that builds the foundation for clinical guidelines troubles many providers.[43] In other areas of medicine where evidence has accumulated through clinical trials, EBM offers legitimacy and support in medical decision-making. With sparse evidence to support the formal documents in trans medicine, providers have turned to creating informal evidence to aid their decision-making in blocking or allowing access to gender-affirming care.

Creating Informal Evidence

Asking providers in one-on-one interviews to reflect on their first encounters with trans patients was fraught with remorse and confession-style stories. Like their mid-20th-century counterparts, most of the providers I spoke with fumbled through the patient intake process and said they did not really know what they were doing when patients sought their help. These providers have been called upon by their patients or colleagues to take what one nurse referred to as "a leap in faith, and a hell of a lot of discomfort" and make the decision to work with a trans patient. Sam, a primary care physician reflected,

> That first [trans] patient walked into my office and said he was a man and wanted to start testosterone and could I please help him. I had *no* idea what I was doing. I sort of felt like we made it up along the way. I don't think I did my best that time. Thinking about it now, after seeing more trans patients, I actually can't believe some of the things I said [to that first patient]. Offensive. I was horribly offensive. But I didn't know. [*pause*] I just didn't know any better.

Trans medicine is often confined to a single "diversity day" in medical residency programs; most providers did not believe that they had the knowledge base to work in it and lacked specific training in the area. Many providers shared that the first few times a trans person sought their help, they turned them away because, as Emily put it, "I just didn't think I could do it. I knew nothing about trans medicine. So, what could I offer them?"

Many providers experienced trepidation in being asked to work with a group of people they felt ill equipped to work with. How might a pro-

vider begin working with a new population of people with no formalized training, and what evidence might they draw from to do so with
competence? These were questions that plagued providers as they considered working with trans people. As Rob, a primary physician, shared,

> Someone came specifically to talk about starting hormones, I suspect and
> maybe, boy . . . uh 10 years ago now, a couple of years into my practice.
> I suspect it was a random call that was taken in our clinic, and the nurs-
> ing staff who schedules people kind of figured that if someone is going
> to work with something like this, they would consider that outside the
> general scope of our practice or the norm of the patient problems that we
> handle. But I said sure, I'm happy at least to talk with this person. It was
> just sort of a moving experience for me feeling like OK, this is something
> that I feel is reasonable within the scope of my practice that I have never
> encountered. I really don't know what to do, but I want to help you.

Not all providers were so keen to work with trans people when first
approached. Some were concerned that because of their sparse knowledge, taking on a trans patient might actually be a disservice, as Anne a
family physician said: "I think it is awkward for patients to have to work
with a provider like me. I may be open minded and willing to try this,
but to say that you have to go to somebody who is inexperienced and
that is the best you can do, that is unfortunate." Brandon, a psychologist
who had worked with trans people to obtain letters of recommendation to begin hormone therapy and who was quickly becoming known
around his town as "the" psychologist for trans people, said that in his
experience, the majority of patients had relative success finding a therapist who was willing to work with them. But he made a clear distinction
that there are differences between finding someone who was just willing, and those who *wanted* to work with trans people. Brandon further
reflected that either way, it was better for trans people to at least find
providers who weren't turning them away but qualified that, "especially
in psychology, I just can't imagine how a therapist would work with a

patient that they feel disdain for. But unfortunately, that is the current state that many trans people find themselves in."

Medical providers called upon to work with trans people came to realize that among their colleagues, they may be the only one who is willing to work with a trans person. Some providers, like Brandon, described situations where as they were learning to work with trans people, they realized other colleagues had "extreme bias around trans people. Like, sickening. And I might not know much about these patients [at the time of first being asked] but, God, some of the things my colleagues would say were just awful." The bias that their colleagues exhibited toward trans patients was an impetus for some to say yes to working with trans patients, as they imagined how their patients would fare trying to work with providers who had disdain for trans people.

Providers who had worked in trans medicine for several years reflected on their growth over time. They shared that while in the beginning they felt exasperated, they eventually learned that for hormone therapy or annual exams, there was not all that much to learn except how to be, as one primary care physician said, "a good person." Natalie, a physician, echoed this sentiment somewhat cavalierly by suggesting that "if you know how to read a blood lab or do an annual physical, you can work with trans people." However, as in other areas of emergent medicine, many providers faced discomfort when first entering trans medicine. They recognized that they lacked knowledge and experience in the medicine, which was complicated by a patient group most providers were unfamiliar with.[44] In light of the goodwill that some providers exemplified toward trans people as they were learning to doctor, and not wanting to "mess up," they still had to face the reality that in their medical education programs, they were not exposed to this particular area of medicine compared to the training they had in other areas. Left on their own, or placed in clinics and offices that had one, or no, other provider who had experience working with trans people, many providers began to construct their own forms of evidence to help them make meaning of trans medicine.

Crafting Notions of Risk as Informal Evidence

"Risk" became a signpost for providers in helping them make meaning of their patient's gender, and whether or not the patient before them was a suitable candidate for gender-affirming interventions. In using risk discourse as a sorting criterion for trans patients, this informal evidence became justification for blocking or allowing access to gender-affirming care while reassuring providers that they were making sound medical decisions.

As I described earlier, mid-20th-century providers needed to demonstrate to their colleagues that they were not "quacks," which could result in them losing their medical licenses. Providers today continue to be concerned about losing their medical licenses, especially those just starting out in trans medicine. It was a frequent question during the question-and-answer portion of health conference presentations. Many professional associations in the US endorse trans care as a medical necessity. However, when medical professionals prescribe hormones for gender transitions, it is considered an off-label prescription because the FDA has not approved hormones for the purpose of gender transitions.[45] As Rebecca, a director of a college student health center, shared,

> I have found that my colleagues are very supportive and helpful, but I think there is a tendency by some people to feel uncomfortable prescribing off label. There is a little bit of the liability concern, and one or two in particular seem to be very [pause] malpractice concerned.

These concerns noted by Rebecca, and echoed in the interviews, are not all that different from the narratives that providers working in the mid-20th century expressed in their correspondence with each other. As Rebecca made clear, the practice of writing prescriptions off-label places some providers in a tenuous position, as they must determine if the discomfort of writing off-label prescriptions outweighs the need of a patient who seeks access to hormone therapy. To protect themselves from being sued by a patient, contemporary providers go through great efforts to minimize the potential challenges they may face to their occupational stability by invoking notions of risk.

While risking their licenses was a fear shared by many, providers voiced more concern with not being able to assess potential risks to their patient's health. In these instances, they acknowledged an awareness of not knowing the long-term effects of hormones. Paul, a doctor of internal medicine, lamented, "There is no head-to-head trial comparison of oral estradiol to estrogen patches. There is no data set about ovaries in patients who are treated with testosterone and whether or not there is a risk for ovarian cancer, or what the risks are for where cancer may develop." As he suggested, there was discomfort in not having scientific evidence in hand to determine overall risk for long-term health problems or what delivery method for hormone therapy was most effective and least harmful to the patient.

Worrying about risk was not exclusive to physicians. Therapists echoed these concerns, as they, too, felt that it was difficult to grapple with how to work in a healthcare setting that had little formal evidence, other than diagnostic criteria, to work with. Mary reflected,

> I think sometimes it is difficult to know how to work with trans people. Is it a mental health disorder? No, at least I don't think so. But what about trans people who have unreal expectations about transition? How do I work with them? Is that a flag? Does that mean we need to develop a longer-term plan? These are questions that I am still not sure how to answer.

With few indicators, Mary and other therapists puzzled through how they were supposed to meet the demands of working with a population of people that were not classified as disordered because of the presenting issue (e.g., being trans) but still felt compelled to offer therapy and support to their trans patients. Without training in gender-specific concerns, these therapists, like their medical provider counterparts, were compelled to begin crafting their own forms of evidence and "flags," as Mary refers to them, to help minimize the risk that patients may experience. Using risk discourse alleviated some of the burden placed on therapists. It helped reframe their task as assessing the likely psychological risks that may occur if a trans person desired to begin a physical transition.

At times, risk discourse contributed to therapists overcompensating by distinguishing normative patients as "real" and those who had symptoms of mental health issues as not really trans. As a result, trans people are asked by many therapists and physicians to be mentally and physically healthy to be considered viable candidates for medical interventions. These implausible expectations for healthiness came to the surface when providers discussed their perspectives on how "co-occurring conditions" were evidence that trans people are not ready to begin transitioning or should not medically transition. At its base, the phrase implies that being trans is, within itself, a "condition." One provider shared the following story about a trans patient during a presentation at a trans health conference:

A 37-year-old phenotypic male patient came to me for hormones and possible surgery and was reluctant to give any past medical history at all. Reports that they made the appointment because another provider told them they had to find care elsewhere, but they couldn't elaborate. Only current medication they admit to is Haldol. I asked why they were taking Haldol and they said, "for sleep." History gathering was taxing and they were very evasive. I asked why they were on Medicare and how they became eligible for disability benefits. Their response was, "I qualified." [*audience laughs*] I question their ability to understand the physical effects. All they could talk about were the clothes they were going to wear. Absolute poor demonstration of the ability to be decisive. This patient didn't seem to have the ability to say to me, "I've got this problem, or this

disorder." I at least need you to be able to say to me that you are understanding and accepting of the fact that you have a medical condition that
is being cared for.[46]

This provider is demonstrating for the audience several explanations
for why the patient should not be granted access to hormones or surgery. First, the medical community has been wary of letting patients
who have mental health diagnoses access trans medicine. This patient
was taking Haldol, a medication typically used for those diagnosed with
schizophrenia, which the provider alludes to suspecting. Based on the
historical concern that trans people might actually be delusional or
have schizophrenia, having likely been diagnosed with this illness created doubt among the provider that the patient was capable of making
an informed decision.[47] Additionally, the provider expressed concern
with the patient's overemphasis on clothing, which was used to portray
the patient as having insincere reasons for wanting to transition. This
is a flipped script from the 1950s, when providers sought to determine
whether or not a trans person could "pass" as another gender, which was
often based on how a patient presented in dress and demeanor.

Beyond the construction of co-occurring conditions in mental health
issues, providers also looked to bioindicators. One nurse related,

> We had a patient who had an A1C (a blood test for glucose levels) of 13
> percent and was pretty hypertensive when she presented at our office.[48]
> We were not her primary care provider. Her gender identity seemed to
> be intact, but the answer was no. There's a lot of comorbidities that are
> unmanaged and unaddressed that make me think she didn't understand
> the relationship between all of these things and taking estrogen.

In addressing the concerns with other medical professionals at a healthcare conference, this nurse suggested that while the patient's gender
identity was not being called into question, the existence of high blood
glucose was enough evidence to halt hormone therapy, as the patient was

not concerned enough for her own health. Taking a hardline stance, the nurse imposed a paternalistic model of medicine by invoking risk, and to help the patient avoid harming herself. Saul, a primary care physician, similarly shared that "if someone is a heavy smoker, that is probably something that is going to need to be addressed before we can start hormone therapy. Or if there is evidence of an unstable mood disorder issue we want to get that stabilized before we do treatment." As providers tried to figure out what their own comfort levels were in blocking or enabling access to care, these boundaries that were crafted around risky behaviors became the evidence for making medical decisions.

Not all providers use co-occurring conditions as a form of evidence to question a patient's viability for medical interventions. As Diane, a counselor, shared,

> I would say that if I have a client who comes in and besides also having gender identity dysphoria, if there are *other* underlining possibilities like major depression and bipolar disorder, I have found that can be a little bit tricky in terms of having that conversation. Because by no means should someone not be able to start hormone therapy just because they have major depressive disorder or bipolar disorder, so for me I have had to sort of finesse the way I talk about that to let them know it is important that, that is being managed as best as possible.

From her individually established evidentiary standard, having health issues is not evidence that the risk is too high for a patient to begin medical interventions. In her understanding, her role as a therapist is to help manage the health issues, as she may in working with any other patient. But a close read of the quote above from Diane also highlights how, as someone who presents herself as "with it" when it comes to gender-affirming therapy, she subtly places being trans alongside "other" mental health issues. And Diane is clear that she would not block someone's attempt to start hormone therapy. But her ways of understanding the evidence of risk are shaped by subtle indicators that she, like many other medical providers, views being transgender through the lens of a condition. With this construction in hand, providers begin building evidence to make a case for working with, or inhibiting attempts, to begin medical transitions.

The Unintended Consequences of Constructing Evidence

How evidence is constructed in trans medicine raises questions about recent trends in EBM as the gold standard for which all medical decision-making should proceed. These new standards are difficult for most medical specializations to meet, particularly emergent areas of medicine.[49] As sociologist Norman Denzin suggested, "Evidence is never morally or ethically neutral. Rather, it is a question of who has the power to control the definition of evidence, what counts as evidence, the best methods to produce the best forms of evidence, and the criteria and standards used to evaluate the quality of evidence."[50] Here, I extended these concerns by offering empirical support to analyze the shortcomings with evidence in EBM.

EBM makes standardizing evidence the ultimate goal. Clinical guidelines and diagnostic criteria further this mission of EBM. However, in the effort to meet the standards of EBM, providers of trans medicine constructed formal documents that narrowly defined who should have access to gender-affirming interventions. As others have cautioned, because EBM is constructed within a medical model, the "problem" to be assessed is transferred onto the patient.[51] In so doing, the medical establishment has furthered their authority, through using the language of science, to maintain control over their trans patients' lives and access to care.

Formal documents have reached mythical proportions as they become codified in writing. For example, the diagnosis of gender dysphoria became real once it was labeled as a formal diagnosis. Over the course of the 20th century, as therapists worked to refine the diagnosis of gender dysphoria, it took on the illusion of evidence-based practices because it was incorporated into the *DSM* and the *ICD* and structured like other diagnostic categories that have EBM to support the diagnosis and prognosis of illness and disease. Over time, the "fact" of a lack of scientific evidence is glossed over as claims to legitimate medical artifacts were centralized in trans medicine.

The paradox of evidence in trans medicine, however, chips away at providers' claims to legitimacy. Further undermining their legitimacy are the ongoing disputes over how to diagnose gender dysphoria, and consensus-based perspective on the steps people should take before accessing gender-affirming interventions. While contemporary medical providers insist that their practices are categorically different than earlier 20th-century providers who worked with trans people, gender norms and implicit evaluations of so-called worthy patients continue to pervade trans medicine as providers parse who should have access to medical interventions.

Beyond using formal documents to construct evidence, we can see the persuasive power of evidence in the ways that providers discuss risk and co-occurring conditions. These medicalized concepts are used to construct evidence of the good patient while setting the foundation for creating informal signposts as standards in trans medicine. Without scientific evidence, providers used risk discourse to maintain the illusion that their "evidence" was established following scientific standards, rather than of their own fabrication. Yet these activities of informal evidence construction have, like the mid-20th-century era of trans medicine, recreated the subtle notion of the worthy patient. No longer within the discourse of "sane" or "insane," the distinction is now more covertly asserted through the language of "risk," which continues to be established based on whether or not a patient has physical or mental health issues or is perceived to develop them when initiating trans-related medical interventions. Through discourses of risk, providers construct evidence to make determinations of patient worthiness. When providers of trans medicine discuss minimizing risk to patients' health, the evidence they construct to minimize risk might perpetuate the very inequalities they seek to avoid in trans medicine.

The consequences of how evidence is constructed in emergent medicine are far reaching and contextualized by the historical trajectory of how an area of medicine unfolds. Mid-20th-century providers of trans medicine constructed evidence to avoid charges of quackery and normalize trans people's gender expression and experiences across social life. In contemporary trans medicine, the focus of normalization has remained on trans people but has extended to normalizing the practice and profession of trans medicine with the proliferation of medical artifacts. Normalizing trans patients remains prevalent in medical decision-making but has been refashioned in more covert ways and sanitized under the guise of evidence-based discourse.

4

Medical Uncertainty

Working with Trans Patients

How do medical providers know when they are making the right decision in the face of vast uncertainty? This is a question that frequently
comes up for providers of trans medicine and others working in new
or not-well-understood areas of medicine.[1] Along with the uncertainty
stemming from the novelty of trans medicine, many providers shared
that they had never met a trans person until they walked into an exam
room and were startled to realize that the person before them was trans.
For most of their careers, up until that first encounter with a trans person, many of the providers I interviewed felt assured that they had some
capacity to work with all of their patients. However, becoming involved
in trans medicine brought into sharp relief the inadequate training,
clinical experience, and scientific evidence that providers repeatedly
described as wanting so they could work more comfortably with this
population. Melissa, a gynecologist a decade into her career, shared the
following story about the first trans patient that she worked with:

> I had done some homework preparing for the visit because I knew she
> was coming. We took some blood labs. I did the history and everything. I
> was going off of the WPATH standards. I still felt kind of weird, like when
> I first started practicing and that imposter syndrome stuff. Like this is
> something that I really haven't been trained to do, but also, these are meds
> that I work with all the time.

Like so many providers who begin working in trans medicine with little
familiarity about this patient group, Melissa did her due diligence in

preparing for the patient visit. Going through the typical routines of taking a patient history and running blood labs, Melissa tried to approach the patient exam as nothing out of the ordinary. But there was a nagging feeling, as she later described, that she wasn't "doing something right." She looked to the clinical guidelines from WPATH for help guiding her through the process of hormone initiation and followed them precisely. But still, in the end, she felt like she was "learning this on the fly and totally stumbling through it." As providers work their way toward clarity as they experience uncertainty in trans medicine, there are multiple strategies they can turn to, such as the guidelines, with the hope that they will feel a little more certain.

But why might medical providers feel such uncertainty when, as Melissa and other providers indicated, they work within medical uncertainty all the time in other areas of their practice? As many of the providers I interviewed suggested, they are asked to make decisions in trans medicine that they feel unequipped to make. Some expressed uncertainty about technical matters such as the correct hormone dose or whether therapy should be oriented around helping clients through a transition process or confirming a trans identity. Others expressed concern that their decisions might not align with professional consensus. Many said that a central point of tension was between how they have been trained to practice medicine and what they are asked to do in trans medicine in bearing the responsibility and authority to decide whether or not a client will be granted or blocked access to gender-affirming care.

The unresolved legitimacy wars that began in the 1950s with physicians and therapists disputing the diagnosis and treatment protocols have also left contemporary providers with fractured knowledge of what criteria and evidence they should use in the decision to proceed with, prohibit, or slow down gender-affirming care. There remains disagreement across the medical establishment on whether being trans should be understood and treated as a mental health disorder that requires psychological interventions, or whether the mind is immutable so the body should be changed to align with the mind. This disagreement, often tacitly communicated by the guidelines and diagnostic criteria, places providers in a position where they are asked to work in ways that contradict a fundamental premise in Western biomedicine that disease is present in the body and remains distinct from the mind.[2] By maintaining both therapists and physicians as responsible for gender-affirming interventions, over the course of the 20th century, the medical establishment has discreetly treated trans identification as *both* a mental health issue and biological illness.[3] Within this dual-mode structure of healthcare, providers of trans medicine must negotiate a lot of uncertainty in best practices for working with trans patients.

Clinical guidelines, as Melissa and other providers like her mentioned in interviews, are a tangible way of helping providers make medical decisions and respond to uncertainty.[4] As one physician suggested, guidelines help providers feel like "they have a handrail to hold on to." Offering stepwise procedures for how to work with trans people, these guidelines inform medical decision-making and can help inexperienced providers to have a document to reference. In fact, most medical decisions are undergirded by a supporting guideline.[5] But the catch, as I described earlier, is that there is little scientific evidence to support the guidelines in trans medicine. As a result, providers of trans medicine spend a great deal of time and effort interpreting the guidelines, which makes implementing them rather challenging.

There is variation in *how* providers used the guidelines for trans medicine to aid medical decision-making, especially the decision to enable or block access to interventions. As I will show, providers invoked two common strategies that had different consequences. Some used the rhetoric of evidence-based medicine and closely followed clinical guidelines to contain uncertainty. This resulted in providers acting as gatekeepers, placing an impossible burden on trans people to be certain about medical interventions, and reifying the gender binary to reflect the assumptions contained within the guidelines. However, other providers flexibly interpreted the guidelines and strategically used them to work within, and sometimes embrace, the uncertainty pervasive in trans medicine.[6]

Although guidelines outline sequences of steps from diagnosis to prognosis, how providers use guidelines can be understood as an interpretive process that reflects providers' understandings of patient populations and how medical decision-making should proceed. Sociologist Jennifer Reich demonstrates a parallel case in her work on parents who opt out of vaccinations for their children: providers who worked with affluent patients had more latitude in individualizing protocols for vaccinations and counseled them differently than providers whose patients had less access to wealth.[7] Part of the flexibility in counseling parents was shaped by a matter of time; parents with more money could afford to pay doctors for specialized care in boutique clinics while those with less money depended on federal assistance such as Medicaid and typically saw doctors who had limited time to spend with each patient. As a result of these structural factors, Reich shows how doctors had variation in following guidelines with the outcome that some patients had more agency than others over health decision-making.

The gender-identity component of trans healthcare raises a distinct set of concerns for how providers of trans medicine use familiar tools in an unfamiliar medical arena, as they attempt to dampen uncertainty. I argue that in using clinical guidelines to support their decisions, providers use strategies in trans medicine that raise broader questions about how the rhetoric of EBM and interpretations of clinical guidelines for medical decision-making may unintentionally perpetuate healthcare inequalities.

Step by Step

Clinical guidelines offer professional consensus on the sequence of steps people should follow to be able to access gender-affirming medicine. Typically, trans people who are explicitly seeking gender-affirming medicine are encouraged to first work with a therapist for a period ranging from a single visit to a six-month period. Over the course of the relationship, therapists attempt to verify that a trans person is "truly" transgender by gaining insight into their client's self-understanding of gender. An ideal patient's gender identity and expression will align with the diagnosis outlined in the *DSM*. Part of the diagnostic process involves a therapist's assessment of whether or not a patient is ready to begin a physical transition.[8] Once a claim to a trans identity has been deemed reliable by a therapist, the individual is referred to a physician to pursue hormone therapy. After a trans person has been on hormones for some time, the guidelines suggest that the next step is for them to undergo gender affirmation surgeries or to change other features of bodies that are commonly distinguished as markers of sex differentiation. At the end of this process, according to the guidelines, trans people reach a golden platform where they are fully transitioned.

The steps outlined in the guidelines suggest a linear pathway in a gender transition, but transitioning is anything but a uniform process that can be precisely followed. Not all trans people seek hormones, and many forgo surgical interventions. Sometimes trans people will have surgical interventions before hormones, or be on hormones for years before even thinking about surgeries, if at all.[9] Coupled with the various pathways to transition, trans people's understandings of their selves and bodies have become more fluid, and "cross" gender transitioning is not always the ultimate goal.[10] Some people opt out of the gender binary but may still seek access to hormones or some surgical interventions.

On the provider side, the nuance in gender identification that trans people bring to the clinic intensifies providers' uncertainty. Where many trans people who seek medical interventions understand transitioning as a lifelong process that is never resolved simply by medicine, some providers have taken the position that any doubt trans people have about medical interventions is a sign that an individual is not ready for gender-affirming surgeries or hormones, or is not truly a trans person.[11] Providers are not always aware of when an updated version of a guideline is released and may use outdated recommendations. Further, with multiple versions of guidelines across various professional associations, and the medical community's ambivalence about which guidelines to follow—or if they should be used at all—there continues to be a lack of clarity about how they should work with trans people. In what follows, I examine the two approaches to guidelines I have mentioned above—close followers and flexible interpreters—to unpack the complexity of how providers in trans medicine use guidelines to respond to uncertainty.

Close Followers of Clinical Guidelines

Invoking the rhetoric of EBM and closely following the clinical guidelines enabled this group of providers to feel more confident in having a justification for the decisions they were making in trans medicine. Close followers described feeling uncertain about how to ensure that a person seeking gender-affirming interventions met the diagnostic criteria for gender dysphoria. Furthermore, without going through therapy before initiating medical interventions, a trans person might not be ready for bodily changes. Close followers also grappled with what restrictions should be in place to help determine that a person requesting gender-affirming care should have access. Trans people have often spent a considerable amount of time reflecting on the decision to initiate medical interventions before entering the clinic.[12] The language of the guidelines, however, suggests that a major component of a providers' role is to confirm that a trans person will not regret medical interventions.

feel responsibility for outcome

Gatekeeping

To help alleviate the ambiguity in deciphering who is ready for medical interventions, some therapists embraced the role of gatekeeper. Sarah, a therapist, in responding to why she felt some measures like prescreening through therapy were needed, commented, "I can't have you wake up on a surgeon's table and say, 'who are you and what are you doing to my body?' That has happened. I know clinicians to whom that has happened." As Sarah described, offering therapy quelled the uncertainty associated with the anticipation that some trans people may regret their decisions. Laura, a therapist who had worked with trans clients for 15 years, echoed this concern with regret: "The deal is you need to become realistic, and have thick enough emotional skin, and when you can do that, I will know that surgery is not something you are going to regret." These providers wanted assurances that, given the magnitude of a gender transition, their patients will not come to regret their decision. As Alesha Doan and colleagues found studying "pro-life" activists, regret becomes weaponized when it is used to propagate misinformation about the effects of medical procedures.[13] From their scholarship, they documented how activists used regret to discredit medical providers' clinical experience in, and knowledge about, the effects of abortions. "Pro-life" activists argued that having an abortion may result in PTSD because of the regret associated with the procedure. As a cautionary note, Sarah, Laura, and other therapists who are overwhelmingly concerned about the potential for trans people to regret their decision may offer conservative-leaning politicians the tools they need to remove trans medicine from insurance plans, and trans identification from federal policies.[14] Close followers used gatekeeping as a tool that benevolently helped their clients avoid regret. However, emphasizing the anticipatory regret of transitioning may unintentionally discredit patients' agency and undermine the legitimacy of trans medicine.

Close followers of the guidelines believed that they were acting in the patients' interest by "doing things by the books," as one physician articulated. For example, one of the steps outlined in a gender transition process is for a therapist to write a letter signing off on a trans person's readiness for gender-affirming interventions. There are situations, however, when therapists concluded that a person was not ready. As Alexis, a social worker, said,

> I have refused to write letters for people, particularly those that want to stop by my office on the way to the clinic. Or those that have mental health concerns, or other issues. But it is a tough function to fulfill. In all other areas of my mental health practice I don't really have to give permission to people to do things.

Alexis's ambivalence about being a gatekeeper was tied to an expressed resentment of some trans people who wanted to drop in for a quick consultation and bypass developing a lengthy therapeutic relationship before heading off to the physician's clinic. On one hand, Alexis and other close followers took their roles as assessors seriously and wanted to ensure they have done their due diligence in evaluating a trans person. On the other hand, as she suggested, giving permission to a client to make a life decision was at odds with some of the foundational premises in therapy. The letters of recommendation from therapists are, in essence, a contract between healthcare providers. But this contract placed a burden on therapists to conclusively verify that a trans person was ready for physical interventions. Physicians also experienced uncertainty about how to assess a trans person's readiness for interventions. Hannah, a director for a student health clinic, said that she wanted to make sure trans clients "are really committed to medical interventions and not coming in on a whim." Because of the long-term implications of trans medical interventions, Hannah thought that involving a therapist would assuage any doubts that she may have had about a trans person initiating a physical transition.

In response to their uncertainty, close followers slowed down the process and asked trans patients to have patience in initiating hormones and coming out to friends and family.[15] Cynthia, a therapist who runs a trans youth group, shared the following scenario to exemplify when and why slowing down a transition might be warranted:

If I get a kid who comes in [to the group] in five-inch stiletto heels, thigh-high boots, and they are like "I'm going to go to school like this tomorrow. And I'm going to call myself by my girl name," I'm like, "Wait wait wait wait wait. Have you talked to the counselor and principal yet? Is there a GSA at your school? Can we please slow down?" And they're like, "Why?" And I'm like, "OK, honey. They don't have amnesia. And you are telling me that you want them to totally accept you, but you're kinda dressing like a hooker and that is fine for Saturday night or if you are a hooker but if you want to be a ninth grader at your high school, think about what do the other girls wear? What do you wear if you want to fit in?" I think there is some naïveté for some of the younger kids who think it's all cool now.

Slowing down, from Cynthia's perspective, helped the trans youth in her group build reasonable goals in transitioning in a manner that made everyone feel comfortable.[16] As she also noted, she was afforded the opportunity to coach youth in how to appropriately dress in their target gender. Though somewhat crass in her description, Cynthia suggested that her overarching goal was to help youth transition as smoothly as possible. Gatekeeping was justified in the spirit of wanting to help trans youth assimilate into cisgender culture.[17] But it also helped preserve the gender order by offering Cynthia a chance to correct any behavior perceived as abnormal or inappropriate by helping clients learn the rules of gender.

Close followers assumed that the gatekeeping practices outlined in the clinical guidelines helped them conform to professional standards while tempering uncertainty. They looked to their medical knowledge about other health risks to calculate the risks that may be associated with a trans person beginning hormones. As Sam, a family physician, shared,

> Somebody maybe has underlying diabetes, or liver problems. Knowing that this is something they are going to have to address, and maybe take care of before they start. That can be a difficult conversation to have with someone, because of course they are ready and want to start as soon as possible. So, to have another delay, but to let them know it is for their own either mental or physical health to address the other concerns first.

Sam used the guidelines to explain to his patients that they needed to resolve other health issues before beginning hormones. In these situations, slowing down the process was justified through co-occurring conditions. Later in the interview Sam shared that when patients have mental or physical health issues it can be "really challenging to know what the right course of action is. I want to help my patients, but I don't want to be responsible for elevated health risks because we don't really know how this stuff affects them." Closely following the guidelines, for some providers, alleviated uncertainty by helping them feel like they were minimizing risk.

Many providers of trans medicine struggled to balance their roles helping trans clients and maintaining a sense of professional obligation to make "reasonable" decisions. This was a troubling situation and contributed to the uncertainty that providers must negotiate. As, Jill, an Ob/Gyn at a university hospital, emphatically stated, "I don't like the idea of feeling like I am holding a prescription pad as ransom. But I am a licensed provider, I do have to work within certain confines to continue to maintain a practice." A limitation of the guidelines is that for those patients who choose not, or are unable, to follow the guidelines with precision, they risk being labeled noncompliant and not ready to begin a physical transition. Shannon, a physician's assistant, shared,

> When I am working with a trans patient, I feel much more like we need to follow all of the steps. . . . If I have a patient that is not super compliant, it's like I quickly get into a zone of "You are making it tough for me to help you here. We have got to follow the guidelines." You know what I mean? I don't know if that makes sense. It is a real challenge.

As Shannon talked through the challenges of being asked to serve as a gatekeeper, she recognized that closely following the guidelines helped provide a structure for her to make decisions within. She also acknowledged that when patients ask for workarounds to the guidelines, her first impulse is to cast her clients as noncompliant.

There are many tools in a provider's arsenal to help guide decisions, including clinical experience and the guidelines. Close followers shared that they were unsure how to apply preexisting medical knowledge and experience, or the guidelines, in the decision surrounding who should be allowed or blocked access to interventions. Most providers I met took this task seriously, and they wanted to avoid the perception that they were flippantly making the decision to block access to gender-affirming care. Closely following the guidelines helped providers, but also created restrictions around *how* they worked with their patients.

Defining the "Truly" Trans

Ann, a family medicine physician, found that soon after her career began, she had quickly built a base of trans clients. Reflecting on why that might have happened, she said that her trans clients "often shared resources and, through word of mouth, referred community members seeking medical interventions to known and safe doctors." As a result, she needed help from other providers in her practice because "sometimes I travel or I'm out sick or can't take on new patients, and I just want my colleagues to be open to working with trans people." She began encouraging providers in her clinic to work with trans people, but many reacted by telling Ann they thought hormone therapy and surgery were elective procedures. As she recalls, "It was scary for them to think about other people saying, 'you didn't have to do this, and you created a problem.'" To help her colleagues feel more assured, she showed them the clinical guidelines from WPATH and "helped remind them that a community of medical providers and experts put these guidelines together and you just have to follow the recommendations for hormone therapy. This isn't that different than what we already do." With some limited success, over time, Ann was able to help her colleagues feel a little more comfortable working with trans people but shared that a lasting problem was their perception of trans medical interventions as elective and "how they were never certain how to know for sure that a trans person was trans or if they were ready for such a massive life change."

There is an implicit expectation conveyed in the guidelines and diagnostic criteria that trans people needed to be certain of initiating gender-affirming interventions. Because the diagnostic criteria emphasize how a person's experienced gender needs to be persistent, close followers transposed their uncertainty by ensuring that their *patients* were "100 percent certain" and were ready for gender-affirming interventions. As I will show, these concerns with a patient's certainty and readiness stand in for providers' attempts to identify the truly trans.

Commitment is a subjective value that reflects the obstinacy of mid-20th-century norms surrounding the credible patient. As Hilary, a director of student health services, reflected when describing how she approached the decision to write prescriptions for hormones, "There are some people who are clearly really ready, and committed, and I don't have any feelings that they are conflicted at all." To be committed signified to Hilary that a patient would not change their mind. Working to substantiate a patient's commitment helped providers feel relieved of some responsibility for patients who are unsatisfied with the effects of medical interventions or back out in the process of physically transitioning. To further alleviate the uncertainty about how to verify a patient's commitment, Hilary and other close followers who abided by the guidelines turned to the therapists to help them decipher their clients' certainty.

The guidelines and diagnostic criteria are resolute about a demonstrable and persistent gender identification to be verified before a person may begin a physical transition but are less clear in directing providers in how to work with patients who might use hormones intermittently. Stopping hormones became an indicator that close followers drew on to assess their patients as not being ready for a physical transition. As one physician encouraged her fellow colleagues in a Trans 101 workshop, "what you are looking to get at is to make sure their gender identity is clear enough that hormones are appropriate." As this physician suggested, one's gender identity should be clear and intelligible to the provider to feel confident that they are certain about starting hormones. By this standard, stopping hormones, or intermittent use, was interpreted by providers as a wavering in the decision to physically transition.

Close followers put in stopgap measures for patients to be verified as mentally healthy before they were granted access to gender-affirming interventions. With no biological tests available to verify a trans identity, physicians relied on therapists to help them clarify the mental health of a patient and to determine whether or not a patient was truly trans. Like their physician counterparts, therapists do not have specific credentialing or training to assess a patient's readiness or certainty about trans interventions. In response, some therapists also closely followed the guidelines and looked for signs to help them make inferences about what criteria should be used to determine that a trans person was certain and ready.

Balancing what is in the patient's best interests with an uncertainty of how that translates into practice amplified providers' uncertainty. Amelia, a gynecologist in a university hospital, said,

> It [healthcare] is always a balance of risks and benefits. I think as long as it is done in the context of the patient, where the patient is the center of the discussion and a part of that discussion. Well, but there are places where I will draw lines. When the risks are too high. But in my own sentence, asking someone who is *truly* trans to spend their life in a body that feels completely wrong is just horrible. It comes off feeling cruel.

Providers are empathetic to the troubling aspect of blocking access to interventions. Some, like Amelia, narrated conflicting ideas about setting up boundaries for patients and refusing to provide trans-related medicine. Using a qualifier like "truly" in relation to a trans person is crucial in revealing a central point in the tension between trans people and healthcare providers. In a medical arena that involves treating an identity, the question is highly contentious of who has the authority, and expertise, to decide if and when a person who claims a transgender identity is "truly" trans. This process of verification—for an identity that has an endless number of permutations—creates turmoil for both transgender people and healthcare providers. Providers may not be able to ascertain with full confidence whether or not a trans person is ready for medical interventions. Most people who make major life decisions rarely know if they are 100 percent certain until they experience the consequence of a decision. It is impossible for providers or trans people to know with such certainty that medical interventions are right for them.

As a consequence of closely following the clinical guidelines, providers unintentionally perpetuate the reproduction of a narrow understanding of trans people, and identification processes more generally, as fairly stable and fixed. The clinical guidelines convey an implicit assumption that trans people should go through the outlined steps to ensure a "successful" transition. In closely following the guidelines, decision-making is built upon the presumption of trans people's certainty and standardizes the assumption that individuals who initiate hormone therapy should never stop.

Assumption of Binary Gender Identification

Clinical guidelines standardize medical decision-making but trans people's self-concepts may not fit easily into binary modes of thought. At the time of the interviews, many of the providers expressed that they were somewhat familiar with genderfluid identities. But integrating their clinical practices to account for variance within gender expression was an evolving process. It is difficult for providers to standardize healthcare delivery when trans people's relationships with their bodies may differ.[18] Alexis, a social worker, reflected, "One of the difficulties is that there is no such thing as *a* trans person. There is this person and this person and this person. When you have counseled for a long time, one of the challenges is listening, openly listening to each person's experience."

The broader medical community's expectations that trans people move from one binary to the other originates from a transnormative narrative that has permeated cultural understandings of trans people since the mid-20th century. This narrative portrays all trans people as having a similar trans experience and presents the goal of medical intervention as helping trans people move from one binary gender to the other, be gender conforming, and assimilate into social life. Bringing nonbinary people into this medical arena creates another layer of uncertainty for providers, especially for close followers. As Mark, a family physician, said, "we are just beginning to understand trans people, let alone nonbinary people." Sam similarly reflected that "some people can get a full transition that fits within their understanding of gender in a binary way. But the fact that their gender is fluid, or falls somewhere between extremes, that is a concept that just blows people's minds." Close followers perceive nonbinary identification as evidence that a person is not certain about initiating a physical transition. Some interpret nonbinary identities as evidence that their client is not truly trans. In response, there were a few close followers who presumed that a nonbinary person needed to shift to a binary trans identity before they should be allowed access to medical interventions.

The existence of people who identify beyond binary gender categories and seek medical interventions runs counter to most medical discourse on trans people and the assumed role of medicine in helping trans people transition. Catherine, a physician, shared,

> A lot of patients talk about how they feel about their gender identity, or how they feel on hormones. But within that, that they may not want full masculinization. So, then it is like "Is this aesthetic? Is it cosmetic? How do we reconcile that with where we just have gotten to? Like, OK, you are saying that you were born like this, but feel like this, let's get you these hormones to get you here." And then we're done, and we clap and we're all really happy [*laughs*]. But of course, we know it is not like that.

As Catherine makes clear, standardizing practices enables providers to feel like they are following a script, and everyone is on board with a plan in place. With the introduction of nonbinary people seeking hormones, there are different considerations and some providers were exasperated with the idea that a person might, for example, "want just a little bit of testosterone to make their gender appearance more ambiguous and would prefer to forgo the development of facial hair."

Close followers experiencing uncertainty wanted standardized protocols to map out a treatment plan for all of their patients in the same way. Nonbinary people's identities ask providers to engage in a different way of thinking about gender while upending medical knowledge about trans people and why someone would seek gender-affirming care. As a result, providers who understand gender in binary terms will face challenges. Brandon, a psychologist, reflected,

> It is way more settling for the therapist to have someone going from something that we have a clear schema for to something else we have an existing schema for. In the land of nonbinary-gender folks, you have to wade through waves and waves of ambiguity. You have to build way more of a relationship with the person and establish a whole lot more trust.

Genderfluid identities represent a landscape on which providers' uncertainty plays out and is made transparent. These identities do not fit within the clinical guidelines for treatment, and this raises a number of concerns for providers—even those who are experienced in working with trans people.

There are contradictions contained within the guidelines that can make close followers even more uneasy in knowing how to use the guidelines in ways that benefit their patients and help guide their decisions. Kim, a family physician, talked through how the guidelines don't account for nonbinary identities, which may result in the denial of care if they see a close follower in the clinic:

> I have to think about what we are comfortable with as a clinic in terms of how we give out hormones. Right? Do we strictly follow WPATH

guidelines, which are much improved in version 7 than version 6? And WPATH 7 does talk some about nonbinary folk. Where I think people got comfortable was with this formula of sex assigned at birth female feels like a man. We will give them testosterone, with the goal of their becoming as masculine as they can get. We have people who are nonbinary and maybe have goals for a physical transition, but don't want all of it. And then the providers get scared that insurance coverage will preclude them [nonbinary people] because the idea is that transition is moving from one to the other and this raises questions in people's minds about whether hormones are even necessary.

As Kim explained, she felt comfortable not following the guidelines to a T. But that doesn't mean that all providers in her clinic shared the same perspective. If the guidelines don't have clear instructions for working with nonbinary people, everyone is concerned that insurance companies will refuse to cover the costs. Sitting on top of that worry is a question that emerges around nonbinary people that reflects onto all trans people: whether medical interventions are even necessary.

Flexible Interpreters of Clinical Guidelines

Providers of trans medicine do not always take the guidelines at face value. As one counselor said, "They are recommendations, they're not proven strategies as the *only* way to do things." With variation in identities among trans clients, some providers recognized it was implausible to follow the clinical guidelines exactly. These providers, whom I refer to as flexible interpreters, were able to embrace the uncertainty in trans medicine and interpreted the guidelines in ways that put patients' needs, and their varied ways of identifying as trans, first. Flexible interpreters were more critical of the assumed benefits of clinical guidelines. In loosely interpreting the guidelines, they worked around gatekeeping practices and were keen to avoid creating barriers to care.

Loose Interpretation of Clinical Guidelines

Flexible interpreters, like close followers, spoke about experiencing uncertainty in their roles as providers working to help people physically transition. Experienced providers expressed dismay with how professional associations such as WPATH have had increasing authority in the practice of trans medicine. They observed how so much attention on creating guidelines took away focus from trans individuals' healthcare needs and the everyday experiences that providers and trans individuals had to negotiate in the clinic. To be clear, most flexible interpreters discussed how initially they would follow the guidelines much more closely because, as Kristin suggested, "You really have to hold on to certain structures because you're so scared. Once you evolve more, you kind of let go of that." For Kristin and other providers, "evolving" was understood as feeling more confident making decisions within trans medicine and identifying problems with the guidelines. As Sarah, a therapist, described,

> I like having standards, which I do not see as laws or rules. I see them as useful guidelines, and they have been helpful for me at a time when I wasn't sure how to balance my will to not to be in someone's way with my clinical ability to see what was going to be in their way if we didn't deal with it first. It was nice that there was the standard that helped me defend that need to a client. I felt like I had backup when I needed that.

Healthcare providers loosely interpreted clinical guidelines in an attempt to balance acknowledged power dynamics with trans clients. Some, like Sarah, were in a gray area between close followers and flexible interpreters. What made her approach to the guidelines distinct from close followers is how she did not perceive them as strict rules. Rather than approaching the guidelines as law or normative frameworks, some providers used them to help guide difficult decisions. Flexible interpreters, such as Sarah, described the usefulness of guidelines most often in instances when they believed a trans client needed to resolve other medical or mental health issues before initiating trans-specific medical interventions.

Molly, a clinical psychologist, conceded that in her role as a psychologist, she had little room to maneuver the guidelines when clients wanted trans-specific surgery. Yet, in contrast to Sarah, Molly placed much more emphasis on her clinical experience and clients' self-knowledge and had a considerable amount of skepticism about the gatekeeping practices outlined in the guidelines:

> I will reference and utilize WPATH as needed. Right? Particularly if I have to work with a client who wants trans-related medical surgery. But in terms of as a clinician, I operate from the fact that you know yourself, you know what you want, you know your body. I am here just to support you in that process, and make sure that you are aware of what some of the changes could be.

As Molly suggested, in instances of contestation between how a provider wanted to be with a patient and negotiating clinical guidelines, some loosely interpret the guidelines to fulfill the necessary but sufficient steps to help trans people gain access to medicine. In prioritizing patient needs, Molly and other flexible interpreters like her referenced the guidelines but eschewed the idea that gatekeeping should be a norm in trans medicine. For therapists in particular, gatekeeping was mentioned as a practice at odds with how they are trained to work with patients.

Other providers mentioned a different source of skepticism around the guidelines; resulting in the need to loosely interpret them. As we saw earlier, the guidelines differ depending on which professional association one looks to for guidance. This lack of consistency can create confusion among providers. As Sean, a physician, said,

> The guidelines have standard operating procedures, and that is not how most patients come in. There are all these different contingencies and you

just feel like at what point do I say this is off guideline, and I'm not comfortable doing it anymore. Fortunately, I haven't had to do that. In any patient population there are people who follow everything you say and there are plenty of people who don't. You don't mess with their gender because they won't follow your directions.

This idea that the protocols presented standard procedures that do not work for many patients was raised by many flexible interpreters. Instead of exclusively relying on the guidelines or finding comfort in closely following them, flexible interpreters were much more explicit in talking about how they brought their clinical judgment into trans medicine to help them work through the uncertainty they experienced. Similar to Sean, Emily, a physician's assistant, addressed how using clinical judgment made more sense to her than closely following the guidelines:

> People are individuals, so they don't always fit into a formula. There are also a lot of barriers to implementing the protocols. A lot of them, for example, call for a ton of baseline labs. If I have a healthy 20-year-old whose cholesterol is probably normal, I don't necessarily need to test it. I think some people might say that you have to draw these labs, this is our protocol, this is what we're doing. But if the patient has no money to pay for all out of pocket then I'm going to use my clinical judgment.

As Emily described, the protocols cannot account for variation in people's health profile. For Emily, and other flexible interpreters, clinical judgment was invoked when they believed that a protocol outlined unnecessary tests or steps.

A major point of contention in the clinical guidelines is that they recommend trans people endure a number of steps before gaining access to medical interventions, such as the "real life experience" where a trans person was supposed to live their life as if they had already medically transitioned, without the aid of physical interventions. Emma, a licensed counselor in private practice, shared, "The expectation about having to live as the gender you are transitioning to for a year before you can start hormone therapy was difficult for me to wrap my head around, and also put my clients in a really tough position." Jill, an Ob/Gyn, echoed this sentiment. She found that applying guidelines to clinical practice was unhelpful because of prohibitive restrictions. But also troubling for Jill was that if followed exactly, the guidelines placed some clients in dangerous situations:

> Even with the first patient, the WPATH standards couldn't entirely apply. At that point [in time] the standards called for the real-life experience for a year. My first trans client was like, "I live in a small town and am a working mechanic. This is flat-out dangerous for me to do this. I just cannot." And my response was, "OK, I kind of wish as the first person I was treating that we didn't have to bend any rules [*laughs*] but we have to bend this rule. You know? I'm with you."

The latest WPATH guidelines no longer require the "real life experience." But some providers with whom I spoke were unaware that new standards had been issued.[19] In contrast to WPATH, the Endocrine Society guidelines have maintained this step as necessary before a therapist can write the referral for a client to begin hormones.[20]

Loose interpretations of guidelines enabled providers to work with trans clients with flexibility and attentiveness to the contexts surrounding their wish for medical interventions. While these providers still grappled with uncertainty, how they described using guidelines demonstrated a process of thinking about uncertainty in a slightly modified way relative to close followers. Flexible interpreters acknowledged that they had to manage a great deal of uncertainty, but it was framed in terms of questioning what was *more* harmful—to treat without knowing if someone was certain about their identity or to refuse treatment altogether. These providers expressed feeling conflict around moral concerns of helping people and a professional responsibility to not harm clients. The notion of "harm" in trans medicine is complicated because it is coupled with the uncertainty of the long-term health effects of medical interventions, given the lack of scientific evidence regarding this arena. Anna, a family physician, said,

> It seems far less harmful to give someone hormones long term and take some risk that it might kill them, where maybe before they were suicidal. And certainly not all trans people are. But for some of them, I think it is absolutely clear that hormones are less harmful. Why would we want to deny that to someone who it will be a life-altering, life changing, life-saving treatment? It is not for me to say to any given person, "Well, you are not quite suicidal, so I don't think it is worth the risk."

Like Anna, many health providers faced dilemmas in their clinical encounters with trans people. Providers weighed how to mitigate "harm" while balancing the uncertainty of the long-term consequences of medical interventions and deep concerns about restricting access to trans patients. For flexible interpreters, the uncertainty of long-term health effects became secondary to meeting the needs of trans clients. Rather than rigidly enforcing the clinical guidelines as a way to contain uncertainty, some providers loosely interpreted them for their own comfort, and to avoid harming trans people through blocking access to gender-affirming interventions.

Working around Gatekeeping Practices

A central explanation for why some providers of trans medicine closely followed the guidelines was to ensure that trans patients were "100 percent" certain of the desire for medical interventions. Gatekeeping creates a structure that asks for trans clients and providers to slow down the process of initiating medical interventions. But in contrast to providers who perceived this as a positive outcome of the guidelines, others expressed outright resentment toward these protocols. They disdained a structuring of medicine that encouraged therapists to serve as gatekeepers and take, from their perception, an unethical position to dictate permission for clients to access medical care. As Emily, a social worker, shared,

> I think the whole gatekeeping thing was a really hard ethical and boundary road to navigate. It was uncomfortable to navigate. I hated it, I hated it. Which is why I am so relieved that I don't have to do it anymore. And, it is not so much of the gatekeeping. It is just a "cover your ass" kind of thing. But it is just hard to be a therapist and create authenticity and connection, when there is all of this suspicion that if your client . . . on the client's part if they say the wrong thing, somehow I am going to stop them from getting what they need.

Reflected in the narratives of therapists and those called upon to assess the mental stability and identify the truly trans, many flexible interpreters found strategic ways to work around gatekeeping. Yet they reserved anger toward the system or other providers, and not trans clients. One recommendation from the guidelines that flexible interpreters were keen to address was the gatekeeping practice of writing letters of recommendation for trans clients. As Alice references below, some therapists were uncomfortable with this process and questioned the function of a letter. She referred to the required letter as demoralizing for clients, and operating against her theoretical orientation toward the role of therapy:

> I have never written a letter that said I recommend anything. I just say I support this person's decision. Sometimes I have gotten pushback for it, but I am not recommending anything for anybody. And I shouldn't be. What authority or what information do I have that would allow me to recommend? I don't want to word a letter in a way that prevents someone from getting what they need.

What Alice describes is that it is unusual for therapists to be placed in such an authoritative position in the lives of their clients. Some therapists noted how this requirement of giving permission for their clients to

begin physically transitioning conflicted with their professional association ethical standards for therapeutic relationships.

Citing the problems with the power dynamic between therapist and
client, Leslie took a different tack negotiating the gatekeeping protocols
outlined in the guidelines:

> I'm of the mind, you tell me who you are. I am not here to tell you who
> you are. I have no right to tell you who you are. You are the one telling me
> who you are. You know, if someone comes in for their first appointment
> and they tell me they want hormones I'm like, "Cool. Groovy. I think you
> should have hormones too." [*laughs*] So let's figure out what we have to do
> so you can get your hormones.

Leslie, like many of the flexible interpreters in the therapeutic community, found humor in how they have to work around the system that is
supposedly in place to protect their clients and their licenses. Yet many
of these providers recognized the irony in that some of the protocols
from the guidelines, and gatekeeping practices in particular, may harm
their clients and erode trust in the therapeutic relationship.

Other therapists reflected on how they felt more comfortable trying
out different language to fulfill the requirements of the letter as they
gained clinical experience in trans medicine. They described writing a
letter that was flexible enough for the person to obtain gender-affirming
interventions but limited in the amount of personal information included. Emma, a counselor, said,

> A few months ago, I started to change the way of phrasing my hormone
> therapy letters. I have moved towards different language, in terms of
> something like, "Client has been feeling in an androgynous place ever
> since they were teenagers." I don't have to say in the letters to a provider,
> "This is a male to female. She is . . ." Over time it was like, "That doesn't
> sound right anymore to me. I want to be able to say this in a different
> way." So, I tried out writing a different kind of letter, and now use words

like "gender variant." The more you learn about these things, you start adjusting based on what feels right.

Many flexible interpreters, like Emma, found ways to subvert the letter to maintain integrity in how they wanted to work with clients. They wrote just the necessary and sufficient amount of information needed for a client to access transition-related services.

Flexible interpreters actively pushed back against the expectation that therapists were qualified to assess the validity of a trans person's request for medical interventions. Some drew parallels to other body practices that do not require a letter of recommendation to frame their perspective. As Brandon, a psychologist, reflected, "If I wanted to get a tattoo and someone told me that I had to see a therapist for three months to make sure that I could really live with it, and that I could cope effectively with having a tattoo on my body, I would think that was fucking ridiculous." Tattoos and gender transitions are uneasy comparisons. What Brandon took issue with was that through premising a therapeutic relationship on gatekeeping, trans people are disempowered. As he suggested, few in the medical establishment would find it appropriate for someone to ask a therapist to ensure that he could live with a tattoo on his body before being able to get one.

Because the provision of gender-affirming medicine, like other areas of medicine, requires a diagnostic label for insurance coding and reimbursement purposes, many providers found ways to work around the guidelines' recommended diagnostic label of "gender dysphoria." These providers acknowledged that even with that diagnostic label, many trans patients still had to pay out of pocket because insurance companies frequently refuse to cover any medical procedures, including routine blood work, if it is coded as a trans-related. Natalie, a physician, suggested,

So far, we [physicians who work with trans people] have had to do a little magic in the way that we code it. But I'm not lying; I'm just saying the truth. Some [staff] people at first were coding visits as gender dysphoria.

And it's like that is not right. I'm checking their cholesterol, their blood pressure. This is a physical. Why would I identify that as anything else?

As a physician, Natalie worked around the system by coding visits for what she saw them to be—physical exams—rather than using a code to indicate that a procedure or lab was for gender dysphoria. In so doing, she protected clients from being identified as trans in their health information records, while also increasing the likelihood that patients with insurance coverage would have their costs covered.

Finally, flexible interpreters were more likely than close followers to approach the question of time with the same loose interpretive spirit with which they approached the guidelines. Many providers described how they had to see a certain number of patients in any given day. This is not unusual for any area of medicine and some scholars have noted how the time allotted for a typical patient visit has decreased in the last several decades.[21] But flexible interpreters acknowledged that rushing through an annual exam presented challenges for some of their trans patients. As Amy, a gynecologist, said, "Trans patients take more time. You have to really build up trust with them and you can't do just a 10-minute visit." In response, flexible interpreters found ways to work in more time to their schedules when they saw trans patients to develop more trust in the clinical encounter.

Unsettled Medical Decision-Making

All of the providers with whom I spoke wanted to do what was in the best interest of the patients. With much uncertainty involved in medical decision-making, there are ranges of options that providers had available to them to alleviate uncertainty. At times, providers relied on clinical guidelines, and at other times their clients' stories, to help guide their decisions. They also used their clinical experience and gut instinct to navigate uncertainty. In light of the vast amounts of uncertainty that providers confronted, they enacted strategic responses in working with trans people. The choices they made may sometimes harm patients, and at others empower them. But providers have some agency in creating rules with which to guide their work.

Some providers attempted to use guidelines as a way to combat uncertainty. In treating clinical guidelines like procedural steps, providers placed the burden of responsibility back onto patients. This was done in order to help providers verify that *patients* were certain about physically transitioning. But in their quest for 100 percent certainty in the clinical encounter, providers constructed barriers to healthcare and reproduced a binary definition of transgender. This "100 percent certainty" narrative also perpetuated gatekeeping practices for trans people seeking transitioning-related medicine. These expectations of certainty put trans people in a double bind. Trans patients must maintain a normative narrative to access interventions and are simultaneously subject to being accused of manipulating the clinical encounter if a provider suspects an inauthentic account of one's gender. For nonbinary people, requesting access to medicine traditionally marked as those treatments that help people move from one binary to another becomes an even more burdensome task.

Within this same structure of trans medicine, other providers flexibly interpreted the guidelines. Confronted with a diverse population of people, some providers found the guidelines too narrowly focused and regimented. These providers were not as threatened by the uncertainty that permeates trans medicine. They were able to more flexibly use the clinical guidelines by loosely interpreting recommendations for medical decision-making and working against systems in healthcare that perpetuate trans oppression and expectations for gender conformity.

In spite of their best efforts to alleviate their uncertainty by using clinical guidelines, each strategy imposed a set of normative expectations upon trans patients. These expectations are established from the historical contexts in which trans medicine emerged in the middle of the 20th century. Providers have relaxed explicit criteria for trans people to be productive citizens who demonstrate their unbridled compliance with the medical establishment in order for them to have authority over their bodies and lives, but there are similar threads that appear in the mandates for compliance and gatekeeping, unease with nonbinary people, and trying to maintain authority in who, when, and why certain patients can access medical interventions while other patients are denied. Even though flexible interpreters might distance themselves from the gatekeeping practices of their close following counterparts, they, too, maintain their medical authority to determine the conditions under which trans people may access care.

5

Uncertain Expertise in Trans Medicine

Three hundred eager medical providers and residents gathered in a large auditorium nestled inside a city center to attend an annual trans health conference to learn more about how to work with this growing patient group. As one conference attendee sitting next to me shared, "I just have so many trans people coming to my office and I really don't know what to do. I don't know *anything* about this." The uncertainty she felt was palpable in her voice. The lights dimmed to signal the beginning of the workshop and the presenter introduced herself as a physician who had worked in trans medicine for over 20 years and would present case studies on how to avoid moments in the clinical encounter when a provider is unsure about enabling access to trans-affirming medical interventions:

> No doubt we have plenty of patients who come to us who can tell us exactly what they want. But they might have other things going on in their lives that they are ignoring. That will alert what I call a Spidey-sense [*audience chuckles*]. When something is not quite right. Because in order to, I believe, in order to adequately treat someone, we are treating their whole self. And although some elements or parts may be disturbing or painful, we need to at least see if our patients are identifying that they need to be treated. It doesn't have to be wrapped up in a box with a bow. But the failure to at least recognize certain things is always a red flag.

The physician proceeded to present several cases that exemplified those moments in the clinical encounter that triggered her Spidey-sense. She offered the audience stories of how she made decisions, interpreted blood labs to check for risks that might accompany hormone use, and identified red flags that led her to conclude a person was not ready to initiate, or continue, hormone therapy. My seatmate looked relieved when the workshop was over, and I saw that on her notepad she had also scribbled down "Check the labs like you would for normal female and male patients. But *trust your gut!*" Part of the discomfort that my seatmate and others new to trans medicine might have when beginning to work in this area stems from the fact that the scientific evidence available is often data acquired from clinical trials on cisgender patients and then extrapolated to trans patients. For example, in working with a trans women on estrogen, should a physician use the baseline range for cholesterol for females or males?[1] As Saul, a physician, reflected, "There are no known long-term effects. No one is saying we're going to take 100 trans women and give 50 of them estrogen, and 50 of them estrogen and progesterone. And then another 50 will get a placebo and see what the effects are. All of our studies are anecdotal as opposed to controlled studies." If the scientific evidence is tenuous and many providers don't have a lot of clinical experience with this patient group, what informs their gut instinct and the interpretive work of evidence?

In this chapter, I examine how providers use different types of evidence to frame themselves as experts. Some of the key characteristics of professionalism and expertise include autonomy and discretion in one's work.[2] Without expertise, the status of an occupation declines and the ability for a working professional to carry out their job is called into question.[3] First, I show how in constructing expertise, providers used evidence to perpetuate gender norms. In the process, they asserted their authority over trans medicine and over gender itself. I also examine how there were two distinct ways that providers negotiated the role of expert in trans medicine. Close followers of clinical guidelines tended to be self-assured experts. Beholden to the tenets of evidence-based medicine, self-assured experts leveraged the guidelines to bolster their conviction of being experts. These providers shifted their uncertainty onto trans people, who then were expected to convince providers that they were certain about pursuing gender-affirming interventions. But, as I will also show, not *all* medical providers play up their expertise. Some providers were open about their lack of expertise in this medical field. Leaning more comfortably into the uncertainty pervasive in trans medicine, flexible interpreters of clinical guidelines were uncertain experts. They acknowledged that new medical fields were difficult to negotiate because of the lack of scientific evidence, clinical experience, and explicit medical training. As one primary care physician stated, "We are doing the best that we can." Uncertain experts attempted to resist the assumptions that shape "expertise" by redefining the basic premise upon which expertise is built. Sometimes uncertain experts were successful, and sometimes their efforts were thwarted by their professional obligations to make decisions misaligned with their patients' desire to access gender-affirming care.

Fake It till You Make It: Constructing Expertise

I enter the convention center and start to make my way through the lobby and toward the registration table to pick up my conference badge. The registration area is loud and full of boisterous laughter. Looking around, I note that while they are housed in the same conference site, there are two distinct wings of the convention center being used: one for the everyday person and one for medical professionals. The area for everyday people—community activists, trans people, and/or allies—is populated by a mostly younger crowd decked out in T-shirts with political slogans or favorite bands and shorts, or skirts with elaborate designs and bedazzled with shiny objects, colorful tattoos, and an array of dyed hair. Moving with purpose, to avert attention from conference organizers, to the other wing of the convention center I enter the medical track and notice a shift in sounds, smells, and atmosphere. It feels like entering a surgical site—anesthetized of laughter and joy, and populated by people who appear very serious, politely sipping their coffees while waiting for the sessions to begin.

On the first day of this annual trans health conference, it is relatively easy to enter the medical track free from surveillance. On day two, the medical track area is more heavily guarded. Conference organizers sit behind tables that create a barrier to entering the medical track. They are not checking people in but, rather, looking at each person who passes through the buffer zone and asking some attendees if they are medical providers. Leaning against the wall and tucked safely inside the medical track wing of the conference site, I note how in the non-medical track wing of the conference there are non-gender-specific bathrooms. In the medical track, the typical gendered conventions apply to segregating bathrooms based on binary genders. This small symbolic gesture signifies that, while the conference is about trans healthcare, nonbinary people are likely not medical professionals.

In a packed room of hundreds of medical professionals, the first session begins: Trans 101. Standing on a stage behind a large podium, the presenter identifies himself as working in a well-known LGBTQ health clinic in the Northeast, and presents his credentials as a nurse and his years of experience working with trans people. He says, "I'm going to present some clinical information. There will be a touch of some social and legal services. But I'm pretty much a medical guy," signaling to the audience his expertise lies in the medical domain. He begins his presentation discussing trans women, and then trans men. His narrative assumes a tone of authority in simply presenting the "facts" and clarifying the biological changes that occur when one introduces hormones into a person's body. Underlying his talk is the presumption of expertise, even when presenting information that is contested by trans activists and social scientists. For example, sociologists of gender have long contended that the expectations placed upon women and men in how they identify as masculine or feminine are shaped by broader social norms.[4] In describing what happens when testosterone is introduced in high levels for trans men, the presenter suggests,

> Mood changes on testosterone are reversible. I just spend a few minutes talking with my guys about what their response is when they become angry. So, if they are people who hit things now, pre-testosterone, they are

going to be people who hit things then, just stronger. Testosterone is not going to make someone something they are not already. It will not turn him into some new human behaviorally.

Social scientists might applaud these efforts to think about the social contexts that shape the effects of hormones on gendered expression and behavior. However, there is a noticeable difference in how providers understand the effects of testosterone on trans men as a social, and estrogen on trans women as a biological, process. The presenter continues remarking on the relationship between mood changes and hormones for trans women: "These patients will have more of a propensity to be tearful, and more of a propensity towards depression. I don't see estrogen as causing it. It exacerbates it." There is a contradiction in the medical community's understanding of how hormones affect trans women and men. On one hand, gender is identified as a social construction. On the other hand, the presenter is describing how hormones will amplify gendered behaviors by drawing on gender stereotypes. From this provider's perspective, trans men are resilient to the effects of hormones, while trans women succumb to the whims of estrogen.

In another conference-like setting, one endocrinologist invited to a grand rounds session for a local hospital to present the newest information related to trans medicine begins his presentation in an authoritative manner. Looking out into the crowd of both new and seasoned medical providers, he asks, "What is the easiest way to change someone's gender?" His response: "Castration." The audience erupts in laughter. The point he is making is that removing an individual's gonads would help that person's body absorb the hormones that were introduced. However, this endocrinologist is insinuating that one's bodily configuration determines one's gender. The endocrinologist is drawing on mid-twentieth-century medical understandings of worthy patients are those individuals who can commit to not having children, as removing one's gonads effectively sterilizes an individual.[5] In further detailing the goal of treatment, the endocrinologist continues to explain that, "For 'female-to-males' the goal is to stop the menses. That's going to be the single *most important* thing that you do. They no longer will have a sense of belonging to another gender." Like the nurse that led the Trans 101 session, this endocrinologist presents information with confidence, while glossing over the complex ways in which trans people come to understand themselves. The message seems to be that trans men inject a little testosterone, add in a swagger while walking, top it off with a hint of musk and some increased muscle mass, and voilà—you have a man! These ideas about gender, understood through a medical perspective and supported by gender stereotypes, become packaged as scientific fact.

Establishing one's expertise in trans medicine expands into expert jurisdiction over gender itself. This situation is somewhat puzzling because, as I described earlier, providers are not trained explicitly in the social contexts and manifestation of gender. However, medical and scientific knowledge is often understood as fundamental truth. Expertise relies on an individual gathering and delivering these truths, even if they do not correspond with reality or are based on false, biased, or interpreted information. When a community of professionals say that they are working with facts, the authority and veracity of those "facts" are perpetuated.[6] Sociologist Annemarie Jutel's work on medically unexplained symptoms similarly highlights how providers who are unable to confirm a diagnosis or lack traditional medical evidence lean on authority and medical rhetoric to support their claims to expertise.[7] We can think of this process as a "fake it till you make it" strategy. Medical providers are uncomfortable with the possibility of not knowing what they are doing but experience even greater discomfort acknowledging it to their patients or the public.[8] The performance of "expert" becomes transformed into the reality of expertise. Some providers of trans medicine have begun to believe the performance.

In the field of trans surgery, surgeons often use gender norms to help them make sense of their patients. The ultimate goal, one surgeon suggested, is to construct bodies that are "as passable as possible." Surgeons presented their "subjects" to the audience through displaying images of people's genitals to show the successes and, in some instances, failures, of surgical procedures. Historian and bioethicist Alice Dreger's work demonstrated how medical providers use the discourse of science in the medical invention of sex categories.[9] Dreger showed how intersex people's humanity is erased in the medical presentations of intersex bodies. Surgeons use photographs with a black bar over the subject's eyes so that one's attention is directed toward the genitals of the person. In so doing, intersex people become dehumanized while their genitals come to define their subjecthood. These patterns are replicated at trans healthcare conferences. On multiple occasions I observed surgical presentations that displayed close-ups of people's genitals before and after surgical interventions and full naked body shots with black bars obscuring trans people's faces. A key difference is that surgeons from Dreger's work used photographs to show how intersex people's genitals should be understood as medical problems, while surgeons for trans people proudly displayed, in the words of one surgeon, "their creations."

Surgeons compartmentalized people into body parts, while reinforcing the notion that patients are not humans, but body parts upon which they craft their notions of what "normal" bodies should look like. As another surgeon shared in reference to gender affirmation surgery for trans men, "If the patient says, 'my penis is too small,' that is true. And also, he cannot have penetration during sexual intercourse. But the patient can have normal orgasm and masturbation."

Traditional gender norms of strong men and passive women have become entrenched in the stated goals of surgeons who work in trans-affirming care. The surgeons I observed also worked from heteronormative assumptions about the appearance and utility of trans people's genitals after surgery. For example, in one surgeon's presentation, he suggested that for trans men, "penis size is of paramount importance for a trans man to feel like a real man," while for trans women, the goal was to create a "perfect and aesthetically pleasing" vagina to serve at the pleasure of her assumed cisgender male partner.[10]

Underlying these biologically essentialist ideas is the reality that this area of medicine is quite ambiguous. In a moment that felt like the front performance moved to the backstage—the place where, as Erving Goffman suggested,[11] social actors divest themselves of the obligations of the performance for a general audience—one speaker reminded the audience during the question-and-answer session, "You have to realize contextually this is weird medicine. We're using non-FDA-approved drugs in some instances, in non-FDA-approved ways." In these moments where providers are teaching each other, the construction of expertise comes to take on great importance to help providers uphold their professional status and legitimacy in the broader field of medicine, and with each other.

Providers sought clarity in how to be experts when their knowledge base about how to work with trans people was not as firm as they wanted it to be. As Emily, a physician's assistant, reflected on the circumstances when she felt that she could not prescribe hormones,

> You know, if you [a trans woman] have had a blood clot before, I can't give out estrogen. I can't. I just can't do it. The WHO [World Health Organization] has this huge chart of what kinds of patients can or cannot be on estrogen and progesterone. It seems to me that I would follow that, because it is issued from the WHO.

In drawing on the WHO recommendations, Emily invoked a well-respected organization to make links between estrogen and blood clots in trans people. But, at the same time, this assumes that this medical knowledge accrued from cisgender people's bodies translates to trans people's risks. And while there is a correlation between estrogen and increased risk of blood clots, the scientific support is unsubstantiated, as these findings assume a cisgender body.[12]

Many providers would think of other medical examples to help them shore up concerns about their decision-making in trans medicine. Jill, a family medicine provider, worried about how others would respond to her decision-making process:

I feel kind of like if you have a heart attack, and you are on a high dose of estrogen, I'm sorry but any provider out there will look at my record and think "what on earth were you doing? The writing was totally on the wall." That makes me feel nervous that like another provider could reasonably look at this and think this was totally heightened risk taking for this patient. And yet I think, you know, if this patient just had ovaries [*laughs*] and produced the hormones that she should be producing or whatever, I wouldn't tell her "well your ovaries are putting you at too much risk because you will control your diabetes, and we need to take them out." You know what I mean? I just feel like . . . mmm . . . it's just tough.

In being concerned with how others would interpret her decision, Jill confronted the lack of evidence to help guide her decisions while also trying to find a middle ground in the murkiness that appears in trans medicine. Unlike Emily, who made a direct connection between the data that exists for cisgender people's bodies and trans people, Jill used her clinical experience working with other patient groups to help her parse her concern with what other people might think.

With difficulty looking beyond the gender identity of their patients, some providers work from a social scientific perspective to understand trans people. As Bill, an endocrinologist, shared,

There is a higher divorce rate, a higher suicide rate in that population, higher crimes in that population, many of them are—if you are transitioning it means that you are perpetually owing money to people. It is a very *very* expensive proposition to transition, and there is always another thing that you can be doing that you want to have done. If you have breast implants, well, you want to have facial feminization. If you have facial feminization, you want to have the bottom surgery. If you have the bottom surgery, you want to have facial feminization surgery. . . . Many of my patients, because they are transgender or for whatever other reason, don't have a lot of money.

Some providers like Bill offer social explanations for the challenges that trans people face. Yet, lacking the tools to critically examine the structural conditions that shape economic inequalities among trans people, some providers fall back on mid-20th-century assumptions where the medical establishment tended to pathologize trans people because they were trans. As Samuel, a physician, similarly reflects,

> It has been my observation, and the observations of people I have talked to, that trans patients tend to have kind of a narcissistic personality style and I have to deal with that sometimes. That is part of the culture. These are people who have had to be stealth for years and lie to themselves often in addition to lying to others. It just becomes part of the persona and sometimes hard to break out of.

In offering social explanations for the character of trans people, Samuel and other providers use their medical authority to construct matter-of-fact statements about their trans patients. They may not realize that some of these statements are offensive to trans people. In their efforts to construct expertise and grapple with evidence, these providers may be unintentionally perpetuating stereotypes about their trans patients while perceiving that they are working in the interests of their trans patients.

Self-Assured Experts

Self-assured experts present information to each other—from Trans 101 workshops to discussions of surgical success stories—in a way that leaves little room for ambiguity in clinical decision-making. As they closely follow clinical guidelines, this set of providers often understand trans identification as a clear pathway from point A (assigned gender at birth) to point B (undergoing a physical transition to the "other" binary gender). As noted earlier, some trans people do not mirror this way of understanding their bodies.

These experts tend to reinforce that the only way to transition is to seek medical interventions and move from woman to man, or man to woman. Any other permutation was regarded with suspicion. In the process, nonbinary people are questioned about why they would want to pursue medical interventions. As one family care physician reflected in how he responded to nonbinary trans patients seeking medical interventions,

> So, when I get a patient who does not have a clear solid gender identity or goal of changing, that physical manifestation of their gender identity, I get concerned about what is my role? I'm the medical person. I'm not the therapist. I'm not the social worker. I'm not the support groups, I'm not the social service people. So those are the folks where I don't know that medical physical transition or stopping of current gender presentation is the right way to go because of the risk/benefit of using these medications. Even if they understand, I'm not exactly sure that medication is the right next step for them.

As this physician shared, his own discomfort stemmed from not being clear about his role in working with nonbinary people. Somewhat dismissively, he presented nonbinary as being uncertain about their gender identities and placed the responsibility on therapists to this patient population figure out if physically transitioning is the right step because from his perspective, nonbinary trans people are not eligible for gender-affirming care. As another provider said in a healthcare conference session on endocrinology, "Give me a man who says he wants to be a woman, or a woman who wants to be a man, and I know what to do. Give me a genderqueer person, and—what is that?"

Drawing on a "slippery slope" argument, some self-assured experts wondered if trans medicine was "going too far" in pushing the boundaries of medical providers' comfort in what role medicine should play in helping people acquire embodied identities. Lisa, a psychologist, shared,

One of the things that we talk about frequently in my professional networks are these wacky surgical requests, or people who really want to
do things we aren't comfortable with. People who want to, for example,
have genital surgery and continue to live in their birth [assigned] gender permanently. I have had people come to me with amputee identity
issues, those who feel like "well if you can do that surgery, why can't
you do this surgery? Why wouldn't you be willing to amputate my
knee, or my leg from the knee because that is my identity. I identify
as someone who is missing one leg." At professional meetings there is
this growing awareness that we haven't solved this thing and put it in
a nice package. It's just getting bigger and bigger, this idea of different
identities. . . . There are lots of people now who feel like they can come
out and proclaim them.

Lisa made clear at the beginning of her description that for those individuals who ask for access to gender-affirming interventions with no intent
of socially transitioning to another gender, there are few guidelines to
follow in handling these requests. Describing this idea as "wacky," Lisa
is upholding a misunderstanding that trans people have the same understanding of their body and reasons for requesting surgery. Lisa then
pivots to discussing a different population of people, those individuals
seeking amputations to realize their sense of self, and who use similar narratives as trans people to request surgical interventions.[13] Like
her mid-20th-century counterparts, Lisa is using worthiness criteria to
mark some patients as worthy of accessing care, if they conform to the
guidelines and her sense of how a patient should understand their body.
For Lisa and other self-assured experts, binary trans people make sense.
Nonbinary people add a new dimension to medical understandings of
transgender,[14] and they rattle the certainty of those who otherwise feel
assured about their expertise in trans medicine.

In confronting nonbinary people in the clinic, self-assured experts
seek to reconcile the uncertainty they experience by passing along expectations of certainty onto their patients. Annie, a social worker, said,

Yeah, nonbinary identification is problematic in the sense of you certainly don't want to . . . If they are still unsure, it makes it as unsure for the provider. I think one of the professional responsibilities is making sure people really understand some of the less reversible nature of some of the treatments. I think sometimes they have very unrealistic ideas like, "Well I will just do this for a while and then I will be OK. And then if I don't like it, I will do this other thing instead."

Portraying nonbinary people as uncertain and unrealistic, Annie, like Lisa, is using a worthiness narrative to make sense of trans people. As some of these providers suggest, nonbinary people who "try out" trans medicine are not worthy of the medical community's attention because they are not demonstrating a commitment to permanently staying on hormones. Yet in understanding nonbinary people from this perspective, medical providers can uphold their expertise and authority by blocking those patients who are labeled as uncertain about their gender identity.

As we listen to providers wade through the uncertainty in trans medicine, Foucault's theory of power lends insight into providers' determination to demonstrate their confidence in medical knowledge and decisions.[15] As a result, self-assured experts regulate patients who do not conform to the norms of medical knowledge as established in the guidelines. For example, as one physician presenting in a health conference reflected on nonbinary people,

I ask my nonbinary clients who are seeking medical interventions, "What are we trying to do, and what is the goal?" If it truly is someone who wants to—for the rest of their life—maintain an androgynous appearance, I can't do that. Living in an androgynous place in the world is great, but difficult. And anyone who is really transitioning will tell you that that's not their purpose. That year starting hormones is hard—socially, for employment, for family. So, I want to talk to nonbinary folks for quite some time about why they would *want* to stay there [in an ambiguous gender presentation] for an extended period of time. I usually let them for three years. There's no evidence to suggest why three years—that's just my feeling. But after that? They need to go back to the therapist, talk about what they really want, and make a decision.

Questioning a nonbinary person's intentions for fitting into a normalized trajectory for physical transition not only helped self-assured experts temper their uncertainty, it helped them accumulate authority and mandate conformity to binary gender expression. As medical providers reroute the expectation of certainty onto trans patients, some patients may be at risk for denial of access to care.

Another physician shared the following story about a trans patient she did not feel comfortable prescribing hormones to:

> All they could talk about were the clothes they were going to wear. Even when I attempted to bring it back around and talk about the potential, even though rare, physical risks for at least them to nod their head in agreement and say, "Yes, I am there with you. Yes, I understand, but I still want to undertake that risk." I couldn't even get that to be verbalized. And absolute poor demonstration of the ability to be decisive. Um, and here's a distinction I use a lot: they were demonstrating urgency.

How self-assured experts think of risk and urgency to obtain hormones is similar to the current public health crisis regarding the mismanagement of opioid prescriptions, and the rise in opioid use.[16] Portraying this patient as seeking a quick "fix," this physician may be interpreting her patient's behavior through a biased lens. The patient raised a flag because they were noncompliant with how the physician wanted the medical encounter to unfold. Denying the trans patient care, she could uphold her authority about making this decision.

Therapists grappled with similar dilemmas in their work with trans patients. Marie, a therapist, described a moment when she refused to write a letter of recommendation for a trans patient because she was concerned that the patient had not carefully considered the long-term effects of hormones: "He was so young, and the stereotypical adolescent impulses in not thinking things through, monosyllabic answers and stuff like that. Not that you have to be an adult when you get hormones. But unfortunately, because of the system, you have to show me a little more thinking process." Marie, like the physician quoted above, continued to explain that she was concerned about younger people seeking hormones because they may not understand the risks and are impulsive. I followed up by asking how a patient can show that they are not impulsive. After a long pause she said, "I don't know. That is a really good question. But this adolescent just would not answer my questions. It was clear to me that he wasn't ready." As she described, gut instinct guides her decisions. Self-assured providers are confident in the decisions they make, but sometimes have difficulty articulating what criteria they use in their gut instinct to determine blocking or enabling access to care.

Self-assured therapists also sought swift decisions in their work with trans patients. Anna, a counselor, shared an ideal scenario for initiating hormones: "just having the patient already have consolidated their gender identity so the patient can walk through the door and it is obvious that we are doing the right thing." I asked what made someone obvious or not obvious; she clarified, "Well, I think that when you have worked in this field as long as I have [21 years] you just see it more quickly. Some clients I think, 'Uh-oh. We are going to have do some work together.'" Deflecting the question of how to assess an obvious trans person, Anna leans on her experience, which helped her justify her use of gut instinct, too.

Some self-assured medical providers become pseudo-therapists as they build expertise in trans medicine. As one nurse said, "When I'm in front of a patient and I'm engaging, or attempting to engage, them I can normally get a sense as to whether or not I need to talk to a psychiatrist [about this patient] in under 10 minutes." Several physicians glibly identified a therapist's role as simply making sure a trans person is "sane," not acting under duress, and their claim to a trans identity is not symptomatic of a mental health condition, such as schizophrenia. Therapists would likely take issue with this characterization by medical providers. But like their medical provider counterparts, therapists also use swift decision-making as a hallmark of confidence and expertise.

Uncertain Experts

Not all of the providers I spoke with or observed in health conferences were self-assured. Uncertain experts were open to sharing that they were anything but experts in trans medicine. These providers offered a glimpse into alternate ways that providers can maintain their expert status but engage in creative workarounds to professional expectations. Like the flexible interpreters discussed in chapter 4, these same providers approached definitions of expertise with flexibility, and in working within the limitations of trans medicine.

Uncertain experts described challenges along the way in reconciling the tension they faced in being called upon as experts while having little evidence to draw from in trans medicine. Many began by first admitting that there was a problem with the lack of scientific evidence and clinical experience. They also made sure to acknowledge that trans patients—binary or nonbinary—were not the source of that problem. Rather, as they suggested, it was the structure of medicine itself that was problematic. These providers were keen to discuss how they had to cultivate a willingness to make an effort to work with trans patients, in spite of their own discomfort. After making an effort to learn more about trans people and trans medicine, uncertain experts sought additional opportunities to gain more training. As a result, many of these providers became sensitive to the needs of their trans patients and gained a growing awareness of how deeply flawed the structure of trans medicine is for not only their trans patients but also medical providers. Finally, with this new awareness, they became critical of those who constructed an expert front. Along the way, uncertain experts redefined the premises upon which expertise is created within medicine. However, while uncertain experts attempted to level the power differences between provider and patient and approached their work with self-described humility, at times they still asserted their authority. As I will show, in spite of their best efforts, they too faced difficulties in their roles as experts.

Amelia, a gynecologist, described the first step in the redefinition of expertise, and recognized broader structural problems in the amount of evidence and uncertainty that permeates trans medicine. She reflected,

> I would say the biggest challenge for me is the lack of knowledge and experience. And some of that is reflective of the field itself, as trans medicine is based on a lot of theory and conjecture. With my lack of experience, I don't always know what to tell people to expect when they [trans people] begin hormones. In contrast, what I have done with thousands of patients, I can really give them a sense of what to expect when they begin a new treatment or prescription.

Amelia had been an Ob/Gyn specialist for over 15 years and had an incredible wealth of knowledge and experience about how hormones effect the body. After all, as she explained, "I work with estrogen all day long." Yet she noted that a major difference between working with cisgender women and trans people's bodies is that trans medicine asked her to extrapolate her knowledge from one area and type of body and try and apply it elsewhere, just as I described earlier with the self-assured providers named Jill and Emily. They, too, described a process fraught with tension in extrapolating scientific data from cis bodies to trans bodies. Jill worried that other providers would look at her decision-making and think that she had made a bad decision in allowing patients who were potentially high risk for staying on hormones. At the time of our interview, Amelia was not entirely comfortable with the idea that scientific evidence on hormones could be applied evenly between cis and trans people. She also described discomfort with the idea that she should have the authority to tell a patient they were not allowed to begin hormones because they were too high risk. As she said, "I know some doctors prevent trans people from hormones because of risk. But we actually don't know what the risks are for trans people."

Uncertain experts also use their gut instinct to help them make decisions. Martha, a gynecologist who has several trans patients, reflected, "Providers don't like not knowing things. To have something within the spectrum of my specialty that I don't know about makes me uncomfortable. Trans medicine definitely falls in that category and I just sort of have to go with my gut and do what I think is best for the patient." In feeling it out, uncertain experts acknowledged that they use subjective evidence to inform their decisions. As Janet, a primary care provider who works in a university clinic, similarly shared,

> I think the biggest thing for me is being in relatively uncharted territory, you know? And not having a great number of people, or resources when I need help. Because there is that balance of wanting to help students, but at the same time being afraid of the potential for causing harm. And that is true for so many things. But because there aren't that many people who are working with transgender students, I don't have the expertise around me as much as I would like.

Like Amelia and Martha, Janet shared that she does not want to harm her patients because of a lack of expertise and experience. Noting the small population of trans students, she suggested that the biggest challenge she faced was the uncertainty that comes with not having a lot of colleagues to brainstorm with when problems may arise. In citing not having expertise around her, Janet subtly conveyed that she does not regard herself as an expert in trans medicine and showed a concern that with this lack of knowledge, she may accidentally harm her patients.

In those instances when providers lack resources or expertise, they must make the decision either to stop working with trans people and refer them out to someone else or to lean into the discomfort and be willing to make an effort in spite of their concerns. Kim, a family physician, reflected on the discomfort that can arise in performing certain exams, like Pap smears, with trans patients:

> We put it off, we put it off, and keep putting it off. I don't believe in holding things over their head like, "Hey, do you want your hormones? We need to do a Pap smear." But trying to navigate those waters where it is just being able to be comfortable with them, and their privacy, and also trying to get to the point where I feel like I am providing them with the best care. It is the same as doing a genital exam on a trans woman. Those are always parts of the interaction that I feel are still not quite as smooth as me doing exams on cisgender people.

By offering insight into a vulnerability that she experienced in knowing that there might be areas of the body that some trans people feel uncomfortable having examined by a medical provider, Kim is taking a risk. Yet she recognized that her patients also felt vulnerable in those moments of talking about exams and tests that needed to be performed on a somewhat regular basis for all individuals. In response to her patients' vulnerability, she tried to reassure her patients that she would not withhold a hormone prescription until an exam or test was performed. It was a delicate balance that she described, and one that self-assured experts might not agree with. For those who are deeply immersed in showing their expertise, they are more likely to invoke their authority and mandate compliance with these exams. Self-assured experts also believe that the decisions they make are in the best interest of their patients. However, Kim, and other uncertain experts, came to a different conclusion in defining their responsibilities as providers. Seeking a middle ground, Kim encouraged her patients to build trust with her, with the hope that they would eventually consent to exams, like Pap smears, that might be sensitive for trans people.

How do medical providers like Kim and Amelia come to retrain themselves to let go of some of their medical authority and cultivate a willingness to recognize their lack of expertise? A crucial step in the redefinition of expertise happened when medical providers began seeking opportunities for more training—either the few formal trans medicine educational opportunities that exist in continuing education programs (such as those offered by trans healthcare conferences) or by training themselves. As Laura, a counselor who works in a community-based clinic, shared,

> I started out working with people in sex work and had a lot of trans women in my caseload. Unfortunately, there weren't many resources. This would've been in the late nineties. There was no one in the community organization who really had any experience or education. I just thought that was unethical, that we were working with a community of people that we knew nothing about. So, I decided I would just start trying to educate myself. I started getting online and reading books. And then, when I felt like I needed some hands-on training, I started e-mailing people and agencies across the country. I would just drive or fly out to other clinics and hang out with them for the day. And I was like, "I just want to learn."

Laura made clear that she felt compelled by a professional obligation to learn more about a community that she was asked to work with in her community clinic. The scientific and clinical evidence on trans people was even more sparse in the 1990s than it is now. Like Kim, Laura also expressed vulnerability in acknowledging the lack of expertise in working with trans people. But within her narrative, there was a sense that in seeking out educational opportunities and learning more about a marginalized population, Laura also began to develop a moral compass that reshaped her perspective on how to work with trans people in an informed manner. In so doing she deprioritized the need to actively show her expertise and sought the help of other clinics and providers.

This set of providers also discussed how they had an increased sensitivity to gender oppression in medical encounters the longer they worked with trans people. As Margaret, a physician, shared,

I sent a patient to someone in family medicine because a patient was having some blood pressure issues. They were unrelated to her trans status. So, I sent her to someone who is listed as one of the few people on a trans affirming medical provider website. So, I thought, "OK, good. This is a safe person." Several weeks passed, and then I saw a note from the clinic visit as I was meeting my patient after the labs came back. She said the visit was fine and she didn't have any problems with it. But when I looked at the note in the system, the patient was referred to as "he" the whole time. I just felt kind of bad. It probably was pretty awkward. Because they [the provider] didn't really know how to handle the situation. But also, how could this person be listed on a trans affirming website?

It is possible that the trans patient didn't even know that the referral was using "he" in the record-keeping, although medical records are easier to access now than ever before as many clinics have moved to online platforms and patient portals that enable patients to view their own healthcare records.[17] Regardless of whether or not this patient was aware of the referral using incorrect pronouns, Margaret worried that her patient was not interacted with in the gender that she identifies as. Margaret later shared that when she first started working with trans patients she "was clueless about this basic stuff" but that now, she sees it all the time. As she continued, "I just think that knowing how to refer to patients using their appropriate pronouns and names can make a huge difference. I had to learn this. I had my patients teach me. But it does matter and shows that we care." As Margaret described, she has accumulated expertise in trans medicine, but thought it was necessary to include her patient's voices in the process.

Medical providers who lean into the discomfort of not having expertise also become critical of other providers who claim to lack expertise but refuse to work with trans people. Some uncertain experts remarked that trans medicine is not "all that different" from other areas of medicine. As Catherine said,

It has been ridiculous just how we have yet to be able to have enough importance to get the people who make the decisions in the same room together, and just say "Hi, we are from [university clinic name] and we have a lot of urologists doing amazing things. We do not expect or think that we are going to have someone who can do a phalloplasty. But goodness, could we have someone who would agree to do an orchiectomy?" Something that is done every day. And you don't need special . . . Could we find someone to do a breast augmentation? Like we are not asking for crazy things. This is utter and complete bullshit.

Catherine, a family physician, balked at the idea that a urologist would not have the expertise to perform an orchiectomy on a trans woman, simply because of her gender identity. There are some differences in trans medicine where expertise is important to preventing patient harm. But some of the mechanics of medical interventions, as Catherine noted, would not be that different between working with cisgender people and those who are trans. An orchiectomy is a similar procedure across gender identities. The meaning it may hold for cisgender men, compared to trans women, may differ. But in treating gender as an essentializing difference where some providers cannot see the body behind the identities, they perpetuate discrimination in health care encounters.

In learning to redefine expertise, uncertain experts focused on how the assumption of vast differences between bodies was a barrier that kept trans people from receiving the medical care they need. "Expertise" was redefined to enable trans people to move through these barriers and establish clinical relationships with medical professionals. But, as Catherine recognized how a urologist refusing to perform an orchiectomy on a trans woman was discriminatory, she also held herself up as an expert who knows better.

The moral compasses that uncertain experts developed brought values into the clinical encounter. Comparing their own choices alongside their colleagues whom they perceived as discriminatory offered these providers the opportunity to assert their expertise. As Collin, a social worker, reflected,

> I think there is a huge lack of knowledge and I think it is appropriate that people would feel reluctant to pick up trans clients, because I think . . . I see so much damage that has been done to people by mental health professionals saying just really dumbass things to them, having no understanding of how sexual orientation and gender identity are generally unrelated. Just coming up with all of these very sort of transphobic and heterosexist ideas that they think are just normal, regular, and true ideas.

In the end, uncertain experts may recognize and even desire to change the systems that they perceive as oppressive to their trans patients. In naming a practice as discriminatory, or a knowledge base as archaic, they positioned themselves as better suited to work with trans patients. This assertion is a form of upholding oneself as an expert, however flexibly they may understand their role in trans medicine. Yet uncertain experts will continue to face challenges as not everyone in the medical community supports their perspectives on trans medicine, nor recognizes their claims to expertise.

Redefining Expertise

This chapter has demonstrated how medical evidence is a social artifact mobilized by providers to construct expertise but can become weaponized when used against people and their embodied experience with gender. Confronted with a lack of scientific evidence to guide their decisions, and often having little experience with this population, providers face a considerable degree of uncertainty in medical decision-making. In teaching each other, providers framed themselves as experts to mitigate their uncertainty in working with trans people and convey their authority and knowledge of trans identities and medicine.

One way this expertise was accomplished was using gut instinct. We read how when trying to assess whether or not a patient was ready for medical interventions, a provider quipped, "It's sort of like Spidey-sense." As a consequence of the uncertainty that continues to pervade trans medicine, trans people are asked to assure providers that they are certain about pursuing trans-specific medical interventions. For those patients who do not, cannot, or choose not to follow the trans norma-tive narrative and seek alternate understandings of their relationship to gender, some in the medical community respond in kind by mandating conformity to normative gender identification. As a result, nonbinary-identified people and nonnormatively gendered trans people become subject to the scrutiny of the medical establishment as they become named and explained away as inauthentic expressions of trans identifi-cation. In using gut instinct as a form of evidence,[18] medical providers may unintentionally allow bias to seep into the medical encounter. In this sense, the tools contemporary providers of trans medicine are using to make medical decisions are similar to those used by their mid-20th-century counterparts.

Within the purview of medicine, an assumption of the goal of medi-cal treatment is to "cure" patients of disease.[19] Trans people present an affront to this assumption. To curb their discomfort, some providers re-fuse treatment or, for nonbinary people, try and persuade them that they are "really women or men." As legal scholar Dean Spade has suggested, "the medical regime permits only the production of gender-normative altered bodies and seeks to screen out alterations that are resistant to a dichotomized, naturalized view of (binary) gender."[20]

But not all providers are so taken with upholding the norms of pro-fessionalism and showing how they are experts in a field that lacks the typical hallmarks of medical expertise. There is a small and growing group of providers who work in trans medicine who challenge the very premise upon which medical authority and expertise is built. Yet the redefinition of expertise is not, as I have tried to show, a comfortable or easy process. As Brandon reflected,

I'm just going to have to tolerate that I don't know what I'm doing, but I'm a better person to do this work than some of the people who were actively pathologizing or judging, or who really want to throw more barriers up. So, I guess I better work to figure out how to be of better service to a population that I feel invested in. All of that had to get unpacked, and all of my anxiety settle, and I had to figure out who I am—kind of as a person in the world and integrate my personal and professional identities together.

The redefinition of expertise can be incredibly challenging to one's sense of self in one's work identities. As a psychologist, Brandon has the training to do deep reflection on questions such as who he is in the world, and what values he holds in more esteem than others. In contrast to those who put such effort into their expertise to uphold their sense of self as medical authorities and to alleviate uncertainty, uncertain experts show us that in redefining expertise, they are also involved in a process of redefining themselves. Like their trans patients, these providers go through a transformative process in their work with trans patients. In the end, they teach us how the institution of medicine is not rigid. Nor is it a monolith. Rather, there are many assumptions that providers bring into their work and it shapes their perspectives of not only their patients, but of what kind of people these providers want to be. In areas of medicine with fraught evidence, providers who are actively working to demonstrate their expertise will find that this is a terribly difficult expectation to meet.

Conclusion

Rethinking the Treatment of Gender

When paired with other social issues that are not well understood, the language of evidence, anchored in science, carries a lot of weight. Consider, for example, the 2018 story that broke on *The New York Times* declaring "Transgender Could be Defined Out of Existence Under Trump Administration."[1] As the authors of this article described, the Trump administration sought to redefine gender as a "biological, immutable condition determined by genitalia at birth." Tasked with adopting a uniform definition to be used across US federal agencies, gender would be determined by the Department of Health and Human Services (HHS), "on a biological basis that is clear, grounded in science, objective and administrable." How they might achieve these definitions, HHS further proposed, would entail defining sex as "either male or female, unchangeable, and determined by the genitals that a person is born with." Any dispute about one's sex and implicitly gender, too, would have to be clarified using genetic testing.

This news story grabbed my attention. I was in the middle of teaching a science and the public course at my current institution and we were unraveling the responsibility of the public and scientific community to each other. Elsewhere, I watched in trepidation as my colleagues stumbled their way on listservs articulating how to bring this issue into their classrooms by offering a balanced perspective that translated to lecturing students on how biological and social mechanisms shape gender categories. Access to gender-affirming interventions is not a philosophical debate. Social scientific scholarship consistently demonstrates that access to care is one of the primary ways to lessen mental and physical health disparities experienced by trans and nonbinary people.[2] Meanwhile, the Twitterverse exploded with virtue signaling around how cisgender allies supported the trans community.

The HHS-proposed definitions of gender and sex did not come to pass in federal policy. However, I caution that this is not a testament to the power of social media or the scientific community. Rather, it is the durability of widespread misunderstandings regarding gender and sex and the misuse of biology in federal policy to further a political agenda.[3] Yet something is amiss in many of these responses, both to the 2018 *New York Times* article and to the more recent unfolding of rulings related to trans discrimination protection in federal policies. The *New York Times* article and coinciding memo, which has drawn the consternation of many academics and public health officials, are replicating some of the same issues that appear in the historical contexts and contemporary realities facing providers who work in trans medicine. As I have shown in this book, medical definitions of gender, at least as they pertain to trans people, are based on an illusory claim to a scientific foundation. As such, there is no balanced perspective on this issue, no neat dichotomies to rely on in the definition of gender, and no clear process for professionals and policy makers to lean on in making sense of gender and sex categories. If sex and gender are, as the Trump administration suggested, plain biological artifacts that merely reside in one's DNA, then the vast uncertainty that medical providers face in knowing how to work with trans people would disappear overnight. Their work would be finished, as there would be no need to offer gender-affirming interventions. Furthermore, claiming that sex and gender can be verified through genetics has far-reaching consequences that are more insidious than the immediate problem presented by asking trans people to verify their gender through genetic testing or genital checks. Glossing over the social components of gender, the Trump administration is drawing from older ideas about gender that wash out gender variation, ignore the historically specific ways that gender is understood, and re-conflate sex and gender categories. In sum, if you can "fix" sex at the genetic level and pretend gender is nonexistent, you can also change institutional policies, dissolve federal funding opportunities, and disregard the persistent structural and interactional inequalities that gender minorities experience.

While the administration engaged in discursive violence against trans and nonbinary people by attempting to write gender identity out of existence, it is also worth noting that this policy announcement came during the Covid-19 pandemic.[4] This pandemic has brought new anxieties to our collective social life, while amplifying persistent social inequalities in healthcare. As of this writing, new infections continue to increase, and the Trump administration's response has shifted from absurd to downright chaotic in just a few months. For example, the country witnessed the president asking a public health expert if it would be possible to ingest bleach to wipe out the virus. Recently, the White House chief of staff defended Trump's claim that 99 percent of Covid-19 cases are "harmless" in spite of the mortality rates ranging between 3 and 10 percent of the US population infected with the virus, with people of color and the elderly having the highest mortality rates because of comorbidities that elevate one's risk of death.[5] Absent from these national discussions on which groups are vulnerable to higher mortality rates because of systemic oppression are gender minority communities. The federal government does not collect this data and refuses to recognize that these groups exist at all.

As the Trump administration engages in misinformation tactics to confuse the public about the severity of the virus, one thing that has become clear to many is that Covid-19 has offered a bleak moment of realness that the infrastructure of the US healthcare system is ill equipped to deal with uncertainty. As I have shown throughout this book, uncertainty presents a number of confounding challenges to medical providers—in how to make decisions and in their sense of themselves as experts. In the current pandemic, how the medical establishment deals with uncertainty has become a part of our everyday existence. News stories are populated by providers describing having to decide which patient is worthy of being put on a ventilator. In some hospitals, these decisions mean that those not selected will likely die. I have shown how, whether uncertainty is surrounding novel viruses or new gender identities, when faced with difficult decision-making marked by uncertainty, medical providers will grasp for evidence to justify their decisions. Sometimes this evidence is accumulated through scientific research. At other times it is clinical experience or gut instinct. These processes become fraught when the evidence used to support medical decisions is biased—either through the interpretive process needed to make sense of the evidence or when gut instinct is filtered through a lens of discriminatory perspectives.

In spite of their best efforts to lean on science because it is assumed to be objective, providers continue to instill values into medical decision-making. This conflicts with a prevailing idea in US society that science is built upon rigorous clinical trials and accumulates into a body of irrefutable knowledge that medical providers apply in decision-making.[6] The assumption of the veracity of science is mirrored in the recent HHS memo that subtly implied genetic testing is a way to verify the "true" sex and gender of an individual. Medical and scientific communities construct evidence when there are no scientific measurements to assess gender identity or verify a transgender (or cisgender) identity. When gender is treated as a biological fact, these essentializing discourses elevate the power of the institution to redefine it within a fabricated reality. The power that is accumulated is fragile, as Covid-19 daily reminds us. As sociologist Madelaine Pape has similarly shown in another domain, mobilizing professional authority through science to make determinations of who can and should compete in competitive gender-segregated sports doesn't make the evidence used to support these claims any less of an interpretive process.[7]

Feminist science scholars have also shown how "sex" is a culturally constructed and historically contingent category.[8] Scientific definitions of sex are always shaped by broader social forces, including the technology available, the indicators used to determine sex, and the stakeholders involved in the definitional process. How the medical and scientific establishment has handled gender is no different. What is often left out of this conversation are the broader consequences of constructing evidence to create professional and political boundaries around "gender" or used to erase it altogether. This book has begun the work of addressing how trans medicine refracts attention on broader concerns in medicine and science in the construction of evidence to justify decisions in the face of uncertainty.

The Consequences of Evidence

Medical providers use the language of science to shore up concerns about the interpretive process of scientific data and medical artifacts. They are trained to think of science and medical decision-making as objective, infallible, and free from human error. Yet, as I have demonstrated, decision-making is influenced by norms, historical contexts, and social factors. Based on the historical record, it should be unsurprising to previously mentioned colleagues and Twitter users that healthcare professionals and policy experts look to science to help justify their claims about social issues. While the evidence that underlies their authority is murky, the knowledge that providers of trans medicine have accumulated through word of mouth in letters of correspondence, listservs, professional association meetings, and healthcare conferences has now become canonized as fact. We can anticipate that these trends in trans medicine, and medicine more broadly, will continue as the datafication of society becomes more thoroughly entrenched across social institutions.

In contemporary discourse surrounding data manipulation, it is taken for granted that there is data in the first place to manipulate. Emphasizing the sociological study of decisions and knowledge, Dan Menchik concluded that studying the construction of evidence should focus not only on "what" knowledge may be used, but where.[9] The findings presented here demonstrate the necessity of social analysis regarding how knowledge is used, and to what effect. The case of trans medicine illuminates how data does not actually need to exist to manipulate it for end-goals, and how "evidence" itself may shift over time to achieve different means. EBM continues to gain prominence as the primary focus for private donations, government grants, and medical discourse. In evaluating the social life of evidence in trans medicine, the findings presented in this book reflect attention on a broader concern that the deployment of evidence goes hand in hand with normalization processes and is used as a rationale for standardizing practices.

Standardization has benefits in treating people or things equally. But one problem with standardizing treatment decisions for a group of people is that variation is subtly conceived of as a problem. In response, decision-makers attempt to erase nuance. In healthcare arenas such as trans medicine where providers have uncertain expertise, the assumptions of EBM unravel when it is used with populations of people for whom it does not, and arguably cannot, apply. A common concern raised by social scientists who study the consequence of evidence in medical domains is that EBM is constructed within a medical model, which places the problem to be assessed, and intervention strategies to be applied, within the individual.[10] While it does help standardize practice, EBM disregards the social, historical, and cultural contexts that define medical issues. For a group of people who define their identities and reasons for seeking medical interventions in a number of ways, trans people may face particular challenges in clinical encounters and with providers who purport to use EBM. Using average outcomes for large populations obscures the heterogeneity of diverse patients.[11] Thus, depending on averages might put some patients at risk, as the medical establishment has difficulty thinking outside of statistical norms. Trans people teach us that the medical establishment also has trouble thinking beyond social norms.

Like many social practices, EBM is a double-edged sword in that the strengths of this model of decision-making can also limit medical providers. EBM helps routinize decision-making. It is also intended to dampen the subjectivity that providers might bring to bear in medical encounters and decisions. But for groups of people that are not homogenous, but are treated as such, the routinization of decisions can make invisible the variety within trans communities and recreate social hierarchies while limiting access to trans medicine to particular groups of people who offer specific narratives that fit within the EBM models.

In navigating trans identities, a lasting concern is how, in teaching each other and attempting to gain legitimacy, medical providers are confronted with the paradox of trying to apply a medical model to a non-standard population. The limitations of implementing standards for a group of people for whom standards cannot apply has been documented elsewhere in the medical literature. For example, Gail Landsman examined the medical community's decision-making processes for crafting guidelines for children with disabilities.[12] This healthcare arena, like trans medicine, has few randomized controlled trials, and data-driven clinical research supporting specific interventions is rare. The authority of medicine trumped parents' intimate knowledge of their children's needs. Landsman's analysis highlights how particular forms of knowledge became transformed into evidence, while others did not. With the medical community's treatment of EBM as *the* legitimated form of knowledge, novel approaches are overlooked in favor of those that are well established.

Narrowly defining, or constructing, evidence as a way to accrue legitimacy and authority in one's profession is not exclusive to medical arenas. As exemplified in other contexts such as school rankings,[13] standardized measures have unexpected consequences, including increased pressure to normalize practices and self-fulfilling prophecies. Standards shape institutions' expectations for behavior to conform to the criteria used to construct the standards in the first place. Clinical guidelines, like school rankings, come to take on their own regulating force in the everyday experiences of providers. From school rankings to predicting the weather, social life is increasingly permeated by an extraordinary emphasis on evidence-based discourse.

The use of medical artifacts in trans medical decision-making with little scientific evidence to support the decisions that are made places this specialized field in dialogue with broader science and technology studies concerns regarding the changing nature of healthcare and the rise of EBM. As noted elsewhere, much medical and scientific knowledge about bodies is influenced by hegemonic ideologies.[14] Like scientific racism in the 1800s that used the science of evidence through the size of skulls to substantiate claims about the intellectual superiority of white people,[15] or sterilizing sexually active women as a mechanism for social control under the diagnosis of feeblemindedness,[16] the medical system may be unwittingly using the language of evidence as a justification for maintaining authority with little awareness of the consequences of such practices.

In using the case of trans medicine to explore broader questions of evidence and expertise, it becomes clear that what is assumed to be objectively constructed "evidence" is still influenced by values surrounding bodies, identities, and normalcy concerns. As social actors, medical providers think about social issues based on what information exists in popular discourse. In medical fields, "trans" is unequivocally defined as people who desire to medically transition from one binary gender to "the other" rather than *an*other gender.

Defining gender as a binary, and building expectations around so-called worthy patients, trans medicine also involves a clash of epistemic ideas about pathology, and one that has very real effects on people's bodies. Defining normative bodies helped medical providers in the 1950s create restrictions around who was deemed worthy to access care. Normative bodies still define trans medicine, although to a much more subtle degree. But, as Elizabeth Grosz reflected, "Bodies provide a locus for the projection and living out of unreflective assumptions. . . . The body has remained colonized through the discursive practices of the natural sciences, and has remained mired in presumptions of naturalness, precultural status, its immunity to cultural, social, and historical factors, unchangeable, inert, and passive."[17]

As I have discussed throughout this book, how medical providers make meaning of trans people and the responsibility of the medical establishment to work with this group of people is in response to broader social anxieties surrounding gender. Creating diagnostic categories and clinical guidelines helps providers define patients worthy of accessing gender-affirming care and shore up concerns about their decision-making as legitimate. When all else fails, providers can fall back on upholding their legitimacy by asserting their expertise and the evidence they have constructed in trans medicine. Providers, like most humans, do not like disorder in social interaction. And trans medical encounters are replete with perceived disorder. Nonnormative gender threatens the social order.[18] As a result, the body becomes a staging ground for the medical establishment to assert proper gender expression, as providers have been trained to bring order to nonnormative bodies through redefining gender and demanding that it belong under medical jurisdiction. The consequences of such practices are that rather than trans people gaining more autonomy over their bodies and identities, medical providers have gained more authority to mandate conformity with a system that does not work for many trans people.[19] As I have documented throughout the book, in spite of their own concerns with the state of trans medicine, medical providers retain their authority as they seek to treat gender because it helps them feel more certain in their responsibilities to their profession, broader society, and in working with trans patients.

Redefining the Treatment of Gender

Just as trans patients are not a monolithic category, neither are medical providers who work with them. There *is* a small, but growing, group of medical providers who are redefining the treatment of gender and how to advocate for their trans patients' needs that moves beyond propagating the assumption that medical providers should have authority over a gender identity. In spite of the little scientific evidence and expertise in this medical arena fraught with professional landmines, and the other challenges that besiege trans medicine, the providers that I interviewed all found joy in their work. These providers teach us how the lasting legacy of oppression in trans medicine and efforts toward gender nor-malization is not insurmountable.

One of the peculiar particularities that trans medicine has had to confront since the mid-20th century is the role of medical providers in working with trans people. The responsibility of therapists has been built on the premise that they should act as gatekeepers, as they are asked to validate trans people's claims to being trans. Even for flexible interpret-ers, the existence of guidelines structures predetermined ways of think-ing about trans medicine, and providers describe either upholding or working around them. But for those therapists who feel deep resentment about being placed in a gatekeeping role, they described that one source of joy in the work they do on behalf of the trans community is to forgo the task of assessing one's gender identity entirely. Instead, as Brandon reflects,

> For younger psychologists that I train, I teach them that in trans medi-cine, our job is to help people navigate the complexities of the impact of social inequalities on trans people's lives and help them figure out how to cope with as best they can the reality of their own lived experience and circumstances. We need to acknowledge that in fact there isn't something deficient, or wrong, with them.

In redefining his task as working with trans people to negotiate the inequalities present in his patients' lives, Brandon, like other mental healthcare providers, is beginning to once again challenge physical healthcare providers' power to comply with a protocol that doesn't work for them. Changing the protocols and shifting attention away from trans people as a problem to fix enables some providers to redefine the "treatment" of gender in a way that shifts the attention to broader social inequalities that trans people experience in everyday life, rather than perpetuating inequalities in healthcare encounters.

Similarly, physicians redefined the treatment of gender as taking on a responsibility to their patients to not impose medicalized understandings onto trans people's experiences or pursuit of gender transitions. Instead, they became advocates through their work with trans people. As Saul, a family physician, said, "I have lost acquaintances who are transgender [because they died], and I noticed they were accessing drugs over the Internet. And I just said that this isn't right. Maybe I can make a difference." Many of these providers gave voice to finding value in using their professional power to empower their patients and help them pursue safer access to medical interventions. As Melissa, a counselor, shared, "Advocacy is an essential piece if you're going to work with the trans community. For me, I just find it unethical that I wouldn't be out there advocating as well." In shifting the conversation to opening up safer access to medical interventions, providers like Saul redefine medical authority as it typically operates in trans medicine—as described throughout this book—and prioritize increasing access, rather than looking for troubling signs that a trans person is not really a trans person.

While I have documented how the language of evidence is sometimes misused to elevate the legitimacy of an emergent field of medicine, my hope is that readers will not conflate this critique with an anti-science stance. Instead, this book shows us the oversight in anchoring one's authority and expertise exclusively onto science to establish professional legitimacy and alleviate uncertainty. I am mindful that just as providers of trans medicine have faced critiques from their colleagues because the science is sparse, so too are providers of medicine grappling with legitimacy critiques that are amplified by disinformation campaigns that have chipped away at the credibility of medical and scientific communities. For example, environmental scholars document how anti-science campaigns began earlier than Donald Trump's ascendancy to the White House. Powerful, usually conservative-leaning, interests have been strategically manipulating information by redefining climate change as a non-problem since the latter part of the 20th century.[20] In healthcare, too, these patterns of disarming the authority of scientific and medical communities through misinformation are replicated, as we can witness with the rise of the anti-vaccination movement.[21] My hope is not to disassemble trans medicine or have the findings from this book misused by policy makers to demand the removal of insurance coverage for gender-affirming care because there is little scientific evidence in this medical arena. Instead, the findings from this book suggest that there needs to be more funding earmarked for the long-term effects of hormones, more opportunities for social scientific researchers to disentangle the healthcare disparities that trans people experience and not face professional marginalization for working in an "offbeat" area of study, and better training in medical schools.

In allocating more resources, I suspect that what we might find is that providers can become nimbler in general, making decisions when confronted with uncertainty and developing better relationships with their patients. As Martha shared, "The more that I worked with trans people, I think I became a better doctor. It's hard. But I learned how to listen to my patients. And as hard as it is, to not make assumptions about them." Instead of siloing trans people and trans medicine into a "specialty" track, all healthcare providers need to be properly trained in working with trans people, which would have spillover effects in more adequately meeting the needs of all patients, learning to work within gender variance, and avoiding the perpetuation of healthcare inequalities. As more providers confront trans patients in their clinical encounters, my findings suggest that providers need to refine their thinking of trans people as a puzzle to solve or a problem to fix. Instead, with little scientific evidence to support choosing one course of action over another, providers need to become more flexible in navigating professional norms and questioning the utility of evidence-based medicine, and to begin placing more trust in clients as the experts over their bodies and identities.

Conclusion

As I was finishing revisions on the first draft of this book, I found myself at a dinner party. Anyone who has written a book can probably verify that attending dinner parties while finishing a book is a horrible idea. The question inevitably comes up: What is your book about? My standard way of addressing this question sounds something like: This book centralizes how medical providers experience uncertainty in their work with trans people. Tracing the social life of evidence in the treatment of gender since the mid-20th century, I demonstrate how the use of evidence by providers reflects broader concerns in medical and scientific communities surrounding the definition of gender. As there is little to no scientific evidence to support medical decision-making, evidence symbolizes the values that medical and scientific communities hold about trans people and gender itself. In spite of this artifact of trans medicine, providers go to great efforts to show how they should be regarded as experts in the field. Creating and using classification systems, diagnostic categories, and clinical guidelines veils how these medical artifacts impose restricted ways of understanding trans people and experience, while helping providers retain a semblance of certain expertise.

My dinner party friend looked perplexed. His eyebrows furrowed and he insisted that scientific evidence does exist in trans medicine. I couldn't possibly be correct. Evidence does exist, he proclaimed a second time. In fact, he just had several students write term papers about the new evidence from clinical trials on the long-term effects of hormones on rats. I paused, feeling my own anger and frustration welling up as I was being mansplained. Before I could ask for him to clarify what he meant by evidence, he said once again, "there *is* evidence now. And, I mean (long pause) their intentions are good . . ." I took a deep breath because I didn't want to get into an argument with a friend of a friend and in someone else's house while we were merrily celebrating the end of a semester. And I understand the place from which he is speaking. As a psychologist, he has a particular stake in the issue and, like so many other providers, is invested in the idea of the progress narrative; the medical community can absolve itself of past harms because things have gotten better over time.

As I have demonstrated throughout this book, having evidence or creating evidence is not necessarily equated with an improvement in decision-making. It tempers providers' anxiousness about their own uncertainty in working trans patients. Many questions remain about what the future of trans medicine may look like, and how medical uncertainty can be resolved in ways other than doubling down on authority, but one insight becomes clear: trans medicine is not a linear story of progress. There are new challenges that providers face in this medical arena and unanticipated sources of uncertainty. With the introduction of non-binary people seeking medical interventions, and a growing population of trans youth, the tools that medical providers have to work with trans people may not easily translate into alleviating these new forms of uncertainty.

Whether we study genes, rats, or humans, sociologists cannot empirically document people's intentions. But we are well poised to address the inconsistencies in how people want to be in social life and how they are in social life. Just as my dinner party guest was likely not intending to mansplain me, nor intending to dismiss the last several years of my work life, he likely cannot recognize the patterns in his own behavior or how his intent and the impact are at odds. Why people are so adamant to insist that trans medicine has improved was a vexing question that helped instigate this project. In the process, what I learned is that analyzing trans medicine is not only about studying a small, somewhat offbeat, field of medicine. Ultimately, the findings from this book draw attention to centralized dilemmas regarding the authority of medicine and science, and how to work in medical areas defined by uncertainty, which is a prevalent feature of contemporary medicine. Within these contexts, power accumulates among those who are interpreters of evidence, and it ominously may spill over into standardizing individuals in the effort to normalize and standardize practices. As more areas of social life rely on evidence-based discourse, decision-makers work under the shadow of evidence, which is shaped by moral imperatives regarding worthy, normal, and productive citizens.

ACKNOWLEDGMENTS

This book would not have been possible for me to write without the support of so many humans (and non-humans, too). I thank the medical providers who shared with me their stories of working in trans medicine. Shawn Wilson at the Kinsey Institute helped me find necessary documents for Part 1 of this work and offered lightheartedness during week-long stretches of sifting through the archives. I also learned a lot through my advocacy work in trans health access and thank doctors Katie Imborek, Nicole Nisly, Ann Laros, and Brad Brunick, who were instrumental in how I came into this work. A portion of chapter 4 appeared in the *Journal of Health and Social Behavior*, and a portion of chapter 5 appeared in *The Unfinished Queer Agenda*. I thank the publishers, SAGE and Taylor & Francis, for granting me permission to build on those publications here.

Countless units and departments have afforded me space to present work-in-progress chapters: Gender, Women's, and Sexuality Studies at the University of Iowa and Appalachian State University; Sociology departments at Michigan State University, the University of Wisconsin-Milwaukee, Wake Forest University, and Coe College; the Center for Gender in Global Context; the Maurer School of Law at Indiana University; the departments of Social Medicine and Anthropology at UNC-Chapel Hill; Duke University's Center for Sexual and Gender Diversity; and the Center for LGBTQ Studies (CLAGS).

The need for scholars to have time to write and think is real. I thank the following for their generous support through fellowships and grants: the University of Iowa's Department of Gender, Women's and Sexuality Studies and the Graduate College, Duke University's Thompson Writing Program, and Michigan State University's Office of Research and Innovation.

I had an unanticipated teaching moment during my dissertation defense where I learned the valuable lesson of how important faculty can be in the lives of early-career scholars. I am grateful for Erin Davis, Jennifer Glass, Karen Heimer, Mike Sauder, and Johanna Schoen in helping me realize the potential of this work and advocating on my behalf. Mike Sauder has also been a constant in my academic life and I remember vividly the moment when I presented at Iowa a few years after I completed my PhD and feeling the shift from dissertation mentor to friend and colleague. I appreciate our lively conversations at the ASA conference and ongoing support. Matt Andersson, Rengin Firat, Chad McPherson, and Mark Walker have been durable sources of support and friendship since we were grad students together. Celeste Campos-Castillo and I have worked together for a decade. I am grateful for your friendship and advice and that we have now reached the place where we can finish each other's sentences.

Mara Buchbinder and I met at a picnic one disgustingly humid day in Durham, North Carolina, when I was completely overwhelmed with new faculty orientation. It wasn't until after I got home that I realized, with great embarrassment, that she was *that* Mara Buchbinder, whose work I devoured and was greatly influenced by. For some reason, she invited me into her writing group, and I have benefited so much from that experience over the years. These folks were also in the writing group and warrant a heartfelt thank you for helping me learn how to write for academic audiences: Jocelyn Chua, Nadia El-Shaarawi, Saiba Varma, and San Juanita García. What a gift!

I have been fortunate to have had many informal and formal mentors who helped me realize the possibilities of this weird world of academia. Elizabeth A. Armstrong and Melissa Wilde were my first mentors when I was a young student at Indiana University; I am indebted for their guidance towards a career in academia. I thank the following people, who have helped me along the way through informal chats or friendly reads: Kathy Charmaz, Kirsten Fermaglich, Clare Forstie, Raina Polivka, Rob Perdue, Jennifer Reich, Teresa Roach, Kristen Springer, and

Arlene Stein. Rene Almeling is a quiet force in my idea development. Her insights, feedback, and support are invaluable to my development as a scholar. I also lean on Laura Hamilton for advice negotiating challenging situations in academia. I appreciate our friendship, which has brought me so much joy and laughter.

Laurel Westbrook first entered my life as an informal mentor and now has become a friend as we trudge through long Michigan winters and meet up occasionally to indulge in tasty vegan pizza, catch up, and swap works-in-progress for friendly reads. Miriam Abelson and I found each other during a 2013 Sexualities pre-conference. We have been good pals ever since, stealing away from the annual conference and going on walk-and-talks to catch a breath and just be human.

My many thanks also to Georgiann Davis for her work that has inspired my own and introducing me to Ilene Kalish and Sonia Tsuruoka at NYU Press. I may have exasperated Ilene with my propensity to add "ize" to many words, but I am so grateful that Ilene took a chance with me as a first book author. Her feedback helped me make more poignant claims throughout the book and her guidance helped me understand the perplexing world of academic presses.

Since arriving at MSU I have met many wonderful colleagues in Sociology and Lyman Briggs College. I have also been fortunate to have reconnected with Amanda Flaim and Daniel Ahlquist, whom I met at Duke. I appreciate our shared meals and porch sits together. Dan Menchik has been a great colleague and has offered incisive comments on my writing and comic relief in matters related to faculty life. I have also benefited from a lively group of scholars in a feminist STS reading group. Wenda Bauchspies, Steph Jordan, and Ellen McCallum are great people to know and be in community with.

The final revisions for this book occurred during the unfolding of the 2020 Covid-19 pandemic. How much daily life has changed. From afar, Jen Ansley's check-ins to chat about gardening, relationships, and writing projects are celebrated. Jill Robinson's enthusiasm for life, laughter, and sipping on bourbon while video chatting is a welcomed occasion.

Sushmita Chatterjee helps remind me to stop working at a decent hour and sends photos to offer a moment's pause for laughter. I also cannot express the amount of gratitude that I have for my pandemic pod people. Melissa Charenko and Greg Lusk are cohort mates and the only people I see in person on a regular basis. They have helped keep me grounded through our weekly several-hours-long walks, check in to make sure I am OK, and support me in countless other ways.

Outside of my academic life, I have the good fortune to have a group of friends whom I want everyone to know because they are so warm-hearted and uplifting: Carrie, D., Kristin, Lindsay, Rain, Ryan, Skylar, Solomon, and Zeke. Many thanks to my family of origin—Mickey, Sharon, Justin, Margaret, Lily, Zoey—who also help me remember to not get so caught up in my work and that there is life outside of academia. A giant thank you to Ileana Haberman for working with me to design the image that appears on the front cover of the book!

This might seem silly to some, but I have learned so much from the non-human animals that have been in my life, beginning with Mia dog, who was with me from the summer before my senior year in high school through the day after I turned in my dissertation. She was my best friend, my non-person person who was always thrilled to go on misadventures and listen to me work out ideas during our walks. I miss her every day. Zams cat became a force to reckon with when I found her sick and dying in the Monroe County shelter my first day as a volunteer. She filled the house with chaos and joy for 18 years. Sketch cat has been with me for two decades, since she was a stow away in my freshman dorm room in 2000. She has been my quiet companion during 13 cross-state moves, 19 different living arrangements, a gender transition, getting my BA, then my PhD, various academic jobs, lovers, and partners, too. Patiently, Sketch sits by my side while I write. She also belly howls from the top of the stairs to declare when the work day is over.

And finally, I cannot write enough about what an influence Ellen Lamont has had in my life. I hope everyone has a person in their life like Ellen. I wouldn't be where I am today without her help, support, love, and soundboarding sessions. She showed me how academic life can be a place for unabashed intellectual curiosity and where lifelong friendships can develop. You have my deep appreciation and gratitude for being such a standup friend and colleague.

My heartfelt thanks to each and every one of you. And a thousand more.

APPENDIX

The Strength of Multi-Sited Studies

For this project, I drew on the strengths of working across several methodological strategies, including archival documents from the Kinsey Institute, contemporary medical artifacts such as clinical guidelines and diagnostic criteria from contemporary professional associations, interviews with medical providers, and observations of trans-specific healthcare conferences. Data collection for this book occurred mostly between the years 2012 and 2015.

Sociologists tend to cut up individual stories or artifacts and stitch these pieces into new stories, with the coherence and context of each original narrative lost.[1] I am trained as a sociologist and gender studies scholar and these fields influence the questions I ask, the place from which I write, how I analyze data, and the stories that I tell. I look for patterns in the data and analyze those patterns in relation to broader social forces. This approach to data also means that how I tell stories is not always aligned with disciplinary conventions. In what follows, I detail why and how I selected the specific methodological strategies for this book.

ARCHIVAL WORK

Alfred Kinsey was a mid-20th-century biologist and researcher who spent the better part of his career making his name in sexological research at Indiana University. Kinsey and his research team traveled the US cataloguing sexual desires, habits, and behaviors.[2] A major driving force for Kinsey was to scientifically study sexual behavior and the physiological responses that occur in a human's body while engaging in sexual acts.[3] He became well known for his 1953 book on female sexuality, which demonstrated that women were more sexually active than the general public assumed. He is also well known for his conceptualization of the Kinsey Scale, which shifted the view of sexuality from a binary (heterosexual and homosexual) to a continuum.[4] The Kinsey Institute is a testament to Kinsey's legacy and efforts to build an empirical base of knowledge on human sexuality.

The archives from the Kinsey Institute contain several collections of correspondence between trans people and providers of trans medicine, spanning a 40-year history that began in the 1950s. During the middle of the 20th century trans people, or at the time people who were referred to as transsexuals, had very few providers to turn to for help with gender-affirming medicine. One of the more robust collections at the Kinsey Institute is the Harry Benjamin Collection. Benjamin met with and treated thousands of patients from the 1950s until his retirement in the 1970s. His collection at the Kinsey Institute is extensively populated with box upon box of all of his correspondence between medical providers, letters of referral, letters from trans people seeking advice, case history notes, and personal reflections. Benjamin was, among other things, a meticulous record keeper. Along with clients' and other medical providers' correspondence, Benjamin's responses are included in the same files. I examined a few additional collections that interfaced with the trans community or medical community, including professional association bulletins, meeting memos and notes, providers' personal notes on trans patients, and informational brochures.[5]

I wanted to understand how the scientific and medical community responded to requests for information, surgical interventions, and hormone therapy. The questions that drove my data collection process included "What perspectives did they draw on to craft these responses?" "How did they teach each other to work with trans people?" and "What assumptions did they bring into their encounters with others in the medical community and with trans people?" Documents from scientists and healthcare providers illuminate scientific and medical discourse on trans people and reflect how providers made decisions regarding if a person was eligible for gender-affirming medical interventions.

What I found in these mid-20th-century letters were deeply troubling accounts of people living in isolation and in fear of being publicly outed by family and community members. They sought clarity on whether they were transsexuals and how to access medical interventions, what the costs may be for such interventions, and whether or not (especially) Dr. Benjamin could help them. Trans people faced humiliation from the legal and criminal justice system and shaming from the medical community, too.

Many of these providers thought of themselves as pioneers in a new and exciting field of medicine. Their experiences are contextualized by massive changes to the gender order that were underway in the 1950s through the 1970s. As such, they were not always aware of the bias they brought into clinical encounters. To a modern readership, the treatments that some proposed sound harsh, punitive, and archaic. As they were learning more about how reproductive organs and hormones work, they tried out procedures on trans people (such as implanting ovaries in trans women) to experiment with surgical interventions.

Elsewhere in the archives, I was troubled to read about how the psychiatric community was also engaged in experimental procedures such as administering LSD as a form of conversion therapy for trans people. Psychologists, meanwhile, seemed particularly interested in the sex lives of their trans patients and gathering extensive case histories. It became clear to me after an exhaustive review of the archives that what was happening in trans medicine in the middle of the 20th century was reflective of broader trends in mental and physical healthcare in the US. How providers made sense of their trans patients was also rooted in concerns regarding worthy and productive citizens in the US after World War II.

Reading through thousands of letters of correspondence and case history notes was challenging for me personally and professionally. I don't think enough researchers talk about the vicarious trauma that we can experience when we are intimately involved in the lives of people we may meet while in the field, or from exposure to brutal treatments in medical histories.[6] But, eventually, a story began to emerge and crystallize through this archival work about the assumptions that medical providers brought into their work with trans people. It would take interviews with providers, however, to puzzle through how while we think much has changed in trans medicine, in fact, the same frames continue to inform the structuring of trans medicine, the uncertainty that providers experience, and how using the language of science helps establish legitimacy in new areas of medicine.

INTERVIEWS

I conducted 23 in-depth interviews with therapists and physicians from a variety of specialties and theoretical orientations, locations across the United States, and work settings. I primarily conducted interviews on the telephone or videoconference calls for this cross-national sample. These are not "typical" providers who just happen to have trans patients. They are a select group of health professionals who have chosen to work in trans medicine.[7]

Many providers in the sample entered trans medicine by way of knowing someone who struggled to find a provider willing to work with them on trans-specific interventions. Only two interviewees exclusively worked with trans people. One provider identified as transgender. Most of the providers were affiliated with a professional association that addressed trans healthcare needs, such as the WPATH or Div. 44 (The Society for the Psychology of Sexual Orientation and Gender Diversity), which operates out of the American Psychological Association. Interviewees were located across the US Midwest, Northeast, and West, and had a wide range of clinical experience and years working in trans medicine.

To identify interviewees, I used a purposive snowball sampling method. I began with my own networks, which originated from my health advocacy work. After interviewing a provider, I asked for them to forward my request for interviews to personal contacts. Providers were generous in not only forwarding my request for interviews to other personal contacts but also posting my request on private list-servs for providers who work in trans medicine and therapy. I deferred to providers' needs for scheduling and attempted to limit the interviews to one hour or less because of the existing challenges contacting and obtaining participant buy-in from people who are medical professionals.

To alleviate concerns regarding my intentions for conducting research, I positioned myself at the beginning of the interview as a researcher who was attempting to fill a gap in scholarship on providers working with trans patients, as there was a dearth of knowledge in this area. What scholarship exists still tends to focus on patient experiences, and rarely examines the provider side of gender-affirming care. I asked for providers to "teach" me about their experiences working in this medical arena.[8] When asked specifically by providers, I was forthcoming about my experience working as a trans healthcare advocate. Many providers assumed that I was trans identified, and if they asked about my identity, I shared that I was a nonbinary trans person. I provided a copy of the interview transcript to each provider and, upon request, omitted any sensitive or personal information. Offering this option held me accountable to the research process and increased rapport with participants. Only one provider asked for an explicitly critical quote to be removed, out of fears regarding potential disciplinary action by an employer. All names that appear in this book have been changed to further ensure confidentiality. I only report the area of specialization because it contextualizes the place from which providers discuss experiencing uncertainty and challenges to their expertise.

The average interview lasted about one hour. I asked broad categories of questions that included beginning with rapport-building "lighter" questions such as the providers' background in medicine and their professional association memberships. Once we had warmed up, I turned to asking questions about the climate of the organizations they worked for, the model of care used, and their experiences working with trans clients. I asked for providers to share with me their typical, and then ideal, patient intake process, how they made decisions to block or enable access to interventions, what flags stood out to them to block interventions, their perspectives on the state of the field of trans medicine, how they grappled with challenges, and specific examples or stories. I ended the interview by asking providers about the sources of joy in the work they did with trans people.

I was nervous the first few interviews I conducted with providers and hyperaware of how this was a significantly different population to interview than the trans people I had begun this project speaking with. Some of my concerns were that providers would offer highly scripted responses. I kept my own perspectives in check, tried to avoid the contentious nature of what some shared with me, and in the end, found myself having compassion for providers. This way of handling the data ensured that I was telling the story with integrity from their perspectives and also the real challenges that medical providers experience in being asked to work with a group of people in their gender identities, and not a biological illness or disease. It is, as one suggested, "rather odd" to be asked to be in a professional space and feel entirely unequipped to work with a group of people. These kinds of insights afforded me the capacity to analyze the interview transcripts from a social scientific perspective and avoid casting judgment.

The interviews were incredibly helpful in illustrating how contemporary medical perspectives are crafted from the assumptions of those providers working in trans medicine in the middle of the 20th century and the continued challenges of this medical field. But there were still gaps in my own understanding. I didn't feel like I had the full story. I decided that conducting observations at healthcare conferences might offer a closer glimpse into the perspectives with which providers engage in their work in an off-script manner. In this way, the observations from the healthcare conferences are more similar to the archival records and letters of correspondence between medical providers. In these spaces—correspondence and conference proceedings—medical providers are speaking to each other, and not always in the same way as they did in the interviews.

TRANS-SPECIFIC HEALTHCARE CONFERENCES

I conducted participant observations in six separate trans-specific medical conferences at locations across the United States over several years. These conferences tend to be populated by physicians and therapists who work in the US, although there are some international providers who are invited to offer a workshop. Surgeons are also present in these conferences, which offered some insight into how surgeons make meaning of their work in trans medicine. But I was also mindful that surgeons are trained in different ways, have different considerations, and are situated in highly specialized fields within trans medicine. These factors inevitably shape how they think about their work and the uncertainties they may carry into the surgical theatre. Some conferences are more open to the general public. Several require participants to pay rather expensive conference fees to attend. Most carry with them the possibility for medical providers to receive continuing education units (CEUs) as an incentive to boost attendance.

I did not identify myself as a researcher while at the conferences. I felt strongly that attending these conferences under the radar would be the best way to gain insight into how medical professions engage each other unfiltered. I dressed in professional academic conference gear to blend into the crowd. Many conference-goers, based on their direct interactions with me, assumed I was a medical student or early-career medical professional.

I audio-recorded conference proceedings and the question-and-answer sessions and transcribed them verbatim. During some sessions, if the audience was larger than 20 people, I took notes on a notepad and composed hundreds of pages of field notes from conference proceedings. In these contexts, taking notes on a notepad did not alert anyone to the fact that I was a researcher. But the more extensive field notes were written after a meeting (or conference session) ended. Each morning following a meeting, I read over my field notes from the previous day and added in information that I had missed during the first pass of writing field notes. I spent around 150 hours conducting observations of trans-specific healthcare conferences.

Conferences present a rich site for examining how providers teach each other how to work with patient populations and off-script comments and observations. I took notes on the information that providers presented in workshops that appeared in the medical education track of the conference, the questions that conference attendees asked, and how panelists responded to these questions. Providers often utilized case studies and patient reports to craft their presentations, which offered a lens into their meaning-making in working in trans medicine and their perceptions of ethical ambiguities that might arise in making medical decisions and the informed consent process. Thus, these conferences helped illuminate how providers teach each other how to work with trans patients, ethical considerations in this arena of medicine, and their professional experiences and case notes in interactional dilemmas with patients.

Through these observations I realized that the public stories that providers told each other were somewhat different than the data from the interviews. In the interviews, providers offered many examples of uncertainty and not knowing the best practices in trans medicine. The healthcare conferences were replete with providers who directly addressed their uncertainties with each other and retold an overarching narrative of progress in trans medicine since the "dark years of the 1950s," as one conference workshop presenter suggested.

CONTENT ANALYSIS OF FORMAL DOCUMENTS

I turned to one last data collection strategy to help round out my understanding of the state of the field of trans medicine. Many presenters in the trans healthcare conferences and medical providers interviewed for this book talked about how clinical guidelines, standards of care, and diagnostic criteria were primary sources of information that helped guide their decisions in trans medicine, and I decided they must be analyzed. As I share with my students in feminist science studies classes, clinical guidelines are rather mundane artifacts. But they tell complicated stories and show the public face of medicine. By that, I mean that these documents are constructed to help guide the decision-making of providers, but they also convey to a broad public the current state of the field and knowledge base of a medical arena.

I examined the diagnostic criteria and clinical guidelines associated with trans medicine from several leading associations. This included the diagnostic criteria for trans medical interventions as outlined in the World Health Organization's *International Classification of Diseases* and the American Psychiatric Association's *Diagnostic and Statistical Manual of Mental Disorders*. I also reviewed the clinical guidelines for working with trans people from the Endocrine Society and World Professional Association for Transgender Health (WPATH).

The analysis of these documents helped me understand how these various professional associations construct evidence in the diagnosis and prognosis of what is now referred to as gender dysphoria, and the assumptions regarding gender that shape medical decision-making. Rather than taking the information presented at face value, I approached them as medical artifacts that symbolically convey the assumptions of medical providers working in trans medicine. Through this process, one crucial thread that emerged was how the scientific evidence that appears in these formal documents consistently failed to meet the evidentiary standards for evidence-based medicine. And the evidence presented in these artifacts, according to my interviewees, infrequently helped address the uncertainty they described feeling or how to make decisions in trans medicine.

NOTES

INTRODUCTION

1 Medical sociologist Renée Fox's (1959) classic work documented how medical school cumulatively teaches students to acknowledge uncertainty and recognize how it might impact patients and physicians, and the range of responses physicians might use for managing it.

2 Cioffi (2000).

3 This is not to suggest that for trans patients, accessing gender-affirming care does not constitute a medical emergency. Health scholars studying trans people's experiences in healthcare have documented how trans people report that it is an emergency (Bakko and Kattari 2019; Davis, Dewey, and Murphy 2016). There is also a considerable amount of frustration reported by trans people with the medical establishment treating gender-affirming care as something that they might pursue on a whim (Castañeda 2015; Poteat, German, and Kerrigan 2013).

4 Giffort and Underman (2016).

5 A study by obstetrician and gynecologist Juno Obedin-Mailiver et al. (2011) found that the average number of hours dedicated to LGBT-related curricular content in North American medical residency programs was five.

6 shuster (2019).

7 Not all trans people seek medical interventions and not all nonbinary people identify as trans. However, in the last decade, there has been a noticeable increase in nonbinary people seeking gender-affirming interventions (Abelson 2019; Garrison 2018; shuster 2017).

8 Douglas (1986).

9 Teston (2017).

10 Timmermans and Berg (2003).

11 Underman (2015).

12 Irwig (2017).

13 Aizura (2016); Poteat, German, and Kerrigan (2013).

14 shuster (2016).

15 Timmermans and Berg (2003).

16 Sackett et al. (1996: 71).

17 Lambert, Gordon, and Bogdan-Lovis (2006).

18 Denzin (2009); Teston (2017).

19 Timmermans and Kolker (2004).

20 Busch (2011); Teston (2017).

21 shuster (2016).

22 Field notes, 2015, East coast trans healthcare conference.

23 Herzig (2015).

24 shuster (2016).

25 Flores et al. (2016).

26 The World Professional Association for Transgender Health (WPATH), which has a leading role in developing internationally distributed standards of care for working with trans and nonbinary people, has acknowledged that "no controlled clinical trials of any feminizing/masculinizing hormone regimen have been conducted to evaluate safety or efficacy in producing physical transition" (2012: 47).

27 Gonzales and Henning-Smith (2017).

28 Timmermans and Berg (2003).

29 Freidson (1971).

30 Abbott (1988); Whooley (2019).

31 Meyerowitz (2002); Rubin (2006).

32 Mishel (1990: 256).

33 Abbott (1988); Bosk ([1979] 2003); Gerrity et al. (1992); Ghosh (2004); Politi, Han, and Col (2007).

34 Poteat, German, and Kerrigan (2013); shuster (2019).

35 Sanders and Rogers (2011); Epstein (1998).

36 Brookes-Howell (2006).

37 Teston (2018).

38 Starr ([1982] 2017).

39 Parsons (1951); Pescosolido and Boyer (2001).

40 Sociologist Donald Light (2010) offers an extensive review of this disagreement among scholars.

41 G. Davis (2015); Timmermans et al. (2018).

42 Epstein (1998); Fausto-Sterling (2000); Paine (2018).

43 Conrad (1992).

44 Breuer and Freud ([1900] 2000).

45 Conrad (2007).

46 Arnaud (2015).

47 Conrad (2007); Dewey and Gesbeck (2017); Link and Phelan (2014).

48 Brown (1995); Conrad (2007); Foucault ([1963] 1994).

49 Armstrong (2003).

50 Berger and Luckmann (1967: 3).

51 Harding (2008); Latour (1993); Cipolla et al. (2017).

52 Scott (1986: 1053).

53 Feinberg (1997).

54 D. Rubin (2012).

55 Butler (1993).

56 Laqueur (1992).

57 Hacking (1990); Foucault ([1963] 1994); Sweet and Decoteau (2018); Fausto-Sterling (2000).

58 Hirschfeld (1910).

59 Money, Hampson, and Hampson (1955).

60 Grosz (1994); Fausto-Sterling (2000).

61 Herzig (2015); Mol (2003).

1. CREATING WORTHY PATIENTS, 1950–1970

1 Hausman (1995); Meyerowitz (2002). Jorgensen was not the first person to undergo gender affirmation surgery, although as she details in her autobiography (1967 [2000]) she was one of the first transsexuals to receive widescale coverage of her gender transition. The earliest surgical interventions for gender affirmation have been documented as occurring in Germany in the early 1930s. Magnus Hirschfeld—medical doctor, author of the first book-length work on the transgender phenomenon, *The Transvestites* (1910), and founder of the Institute for Sexual Science—mentored early-career doctors in sexual variation. His mentorship had far-reaching effects. Eugene Steinach was a friend of Hirschfeld and was the first endocrinologist to document the effects of testosterone and estrogen in 1912. Harry Benjamin moved from Germany to the United States and became a leading authority and catalyst for the medical community's involvement in hormone therapy and surgery for transsexuals in the 1950s (Stryker 2008).

2 Serlin (1995).

3 Coontz ([1992] 2016).

4 McKinlay and Marceau (2002); Timmermans and Oh (2010).

5 Sandra Harding (2008) and other science and technology studies scholars (Haraway 1991; Latour 1993) have extensively documented how medical and scientific communities eschew the influence of culture on the scientific process and medical encounters, but decades of scholarship have made clear that culture and science are deeply intertwined and mutually constituted.

6 Spade (2006).

7 Harry Benjamin Foundation, 1965. "Meeting Notes." Box 23, Harry Benjamin Collection, Kinsey Institute, Bloomington, IN.

8 Author concealed, 1961. "Letter from surgeon to provider." Box 3, Harry Benjamin Collection, Kinsey Institute, Bloomington, IN.

9 Starr ([1982] 2017); Timmermans and Oh (2010).

10 Winnick (2005).

11 In this quick rendition of the rise of professional power in American medicine, I do not mean to indicate that this was a linear history of "progress" made through advancements in knowledge. For a much more detailed history of the rise of professional power among allopaths during the 19th and 20th centuries, see Owen Whooley's (2013) work.

12 Pescosolido and Boyer (2001).

13 McKinlay and Marceau (2002).

14 Harry Benjamin, 1962. "Letter to surgeon." Box 3, Harry Benjamin Collection, Kinsey Institute, Bloomington, IN.

15 Author concealed, 1964. "Letter from provider to Benjamin." Box 8, Harry Benjamin Collection, Kinsey Institute, Bloomington, IN.

16 Author concealed, 1958. "Letter from surgeon to Benjamin." Box 3, Harry Benjamin Collection, Kinsey Institute, Bloomington, IN.

17 Harry Benjamin Foundation, 1965. "Meeting Notes." Box 23, Harry Benjamin Collection, Kinsey Institute, Bloomington, IN.

18 Harry Benjamin, 1962. "Letter to surgeon." Box 3, Harry Benjamin Collection, Kinsey Institute, Bloomington, IN.

19 Author concealed. 1969. "Letter from physician to the Erickson Educational Foundation." Box 3, Harry Benjamin Collection, Kinsey Institute, Bloomington, IN.

20 Author concealed. 1962. "Letter from surgeon to Benjamin." Box 3, Harry Benjamin Collection, Kinsey Institute, Bloomington, IN.

21 Eskridge (1999).

22 Meyerowitz (2002).

23 Stryker and Sullivan (2009).

24 Harry Benjamin, 1962. "Letter to surgeon." Box 3, Harry Benjamin Collection, Kinsey Institute, Bloomington, IN.

25 Harry Benjamin, 1962. "Letter to surgeon." Box 3, Harry Benjamin Collection, Kinsey Institute, Bloomington, IN.

26 Stark (2012).

27 Author concealed, 1964. "Letter from surgeon to provider." Box 3, Harry Benjamin Collection, Kinsey Institute, Bloomington, IN.

28 Harry Benjamin, 1962. "Letter to surgeon." Box 3, Harry Benjamin Collection, Kinsey Institute, Bloomington, IN.

29 Author concealed, 1959. "Letter from patient to Benjamin." Box 6, Harry Benjamin Collection, Kinsey Institute, Bloomington, IN. The current guidelines suggest an average weekly dose of testosterone is anywhere between 20 and 100 milligrams (Deutsch n.d.).

30 Author concealed, 1970. "Letter from patient to Benjamin." Box 4, Harry Benjamin Collection, Kinsey Institute, Bloomington, IN.

31 Author concealed, 1964. "Letter from doctor to Benjamin." Box 3, Harry Benjamin Collection, Kinsey Institute, Bloomington, IN.

32 Bettcher (2007).

33 Author concealed, 1972. "Letter from patient to Johns Hopkins Gender Identity Clinic." Box 3, Harry Benjamin Collection, Kinsey Institute, Bloomington, IN.

34 Bergstrand and Jasper (2018).

35 In mid-20th-century medical understandings, there were only two genders, and all trans people were assumed to want to transition from woman to man or from man to woman.

36 Author concealed, 1962. "Letter from doctor to provider." Box 3, Harry Benjamin Collection, Kinsey Institute, Bloomington, IN.

37 Harry Benjamin, 1966. "Letter to patient." Box 4, Harry Benjamin Collection, Kinsey Institute, Bloomington, IN.

38 Author concealed, 1957. "Letter from surgeon to Benjamin." Box 23, Harry Benjamin Collection, Kinsey Institute, Bloomington, IN.

39 The Health Insurance Portability and Accountability Act (HIPAA) was enacted on August 21, 1996. Thus, it was not an unusual request for a medical provider to require trans people to disclose to their families that they were seeking gender-related surgeries.

40 Author concealed, 1968. "Letter from patient to provider." Box 7, Harry Benjamin Collection, Kinsey Institute, Bloomington, IN.

41 Stryker (2008).

42 Harry Benjamin, 1954. "Letter from Benjamin to patient." Box 7, Harry Benjamin Collection, Kinsey Institute, Bloomington, IN.

43 McKinlay and Marceau (2002).

44 Casper (1998); Fordyce (2013).

45 Author concealed, 1958. "Letter from provider to provider." Box 3, Harry Benjamin Collection, Kinsey Institute, Bloomington, IN.

46 Spade (2006).

47 Author concealed, 1966. "Letter from doctor to Benjamin." Box 6, Harry Benjamin Collection, Kinsey Institute. Bloomington, IN.

48 Author concealed, 1960. "Letter from surgeon to Benjamin." Box 3, Harry Benjamin Collection, Kinsey Institute, Bloomington, IN.

49 Author concealed, 1968. "Letter from doctor to provider." Box 3, Harry Benjamin Collection, Kinsey Institute, Bloomington, IN.

50 Author concealed, 1958. "Letter from surgeon to provider." Box 3, Harry Benjamin Collection, Kinsey Institute, Bloomington, IN.

51 Author concealed, 1975. "Letter from doctor to patient." Box 4, Harry Benjamin Collection, Kinsey Institute, Bloomington, IN.

52 Author concealed, 1958. "Letter from surgeon to Benjamin." Box 3, Harry Benjamin Collection, Kinsey Institute, Bloomington, IN.

53 Author concealed, 1974. "Medical report sent to doctor for referral notes." Box 5, Harry Benjamin Collection, Kinsey Institute, Bloomington, IN.

54 Author concealed, 1967. "Letter from surgeon to Benjamin." Box 6, Harry Benjamin Collection, Kinsey Institute, Bloomington, IN.

55 This test has been referred to as the "real life experience" or "real life test." I discuss in later chapters how this standard was established in the 1960s, codified in the clinical guidelines for transgender care, and maintained in the guidelines until 2012.

56 Harry Benjamin, 1962. "Letter from Benjamin to patient." Box 4, Harry Benjamin Collection, Kinsey Institute, Bloomington, IN.

57 Author concealed, 1962. "Letter from patient to Benjamin." Box 4, Harry Benjamin Collection, Kinsey Institute, Bloomington, IN.

58 Author concealed, 1963. "Letter from patient to Benjamin." Box 4, Harry Benjamin Collection, Kinsey Institute, Bloomington, IN.

59 Harry Benjamin, 1964. "Letter from Benjamin to patient." Box 4, Harry Benjamin Collection, Kinsey Institute, Bloomington, IN.

60 Prosser (1998).

61 As others have noted, the medical community's attention on trans men is less robust in the archives on the mid-20th-century trans phenomenon (Cromwell 1999). It is difficult to discern what the appearance standards were for trans men. From the archives available at the Kinsey Institute, it is clear that trans men were supposed to uphold traditional masculinity and work in occupations traditionally marked as men's work.

62 Harry Benjamin, 1955. "Letter to patient." Box 5, Harry Benjamin Collection, Kinsey Institute, Bloomington, IN.

63 Author concealed, 1959. "Letter from surgeon to Benjamin." Box 3, Harry Benjamin Collection, Kinsey Institute, Bloomington, IN.

64 L. Davis (1995).

65 Garland-Thomson (1997).

66 G. Davis (2015); Karkazis (2008).

67 Hacking (1990); Sweet and Decoteau (2018).

68 Author concealed, 1967. "Letter from scientist to Benjamin." Box 23, Harry Benjamin Collection, Kinsey Institute, Bloomington, IN.

69 Harry Benjamin, 1968. "Letter from Benjamin to attorney." Box 8, Harry Benjamin Collection, Kinsey Institute, Bloomington, IN.

70 Harry Benjamin, 1969. "Letter from Benjamin to wife of trans person." Box 7, Harry Benjamin Collection, Kinsey Institute, Bloomington, IN.

71 Author concealed, 1961. "Letter to surgeon." Box 3, Harry Benjamin Collection, Kinsey Institute, Bloomington, IN.

72 Harry Benjamin, 1961. "Letter to doctor." Box 3, Harry Benjamin Collection, Kinsey Institute, Bloomington, IN.

73 Irving (2008).

74 Harry Benjamin, 1958. "Letter to doctor." Box 3, Harry Benjamin Collection, Kinsey Institute, Bloomington, IN.

75 Author concealed, 1968. "Letter to doctor." Box 6, Harry Benjamin Collection, Kinsey Institute, Bloomington, IN.

76 Author concealed, 1968. "Letter to patient." Box 6, Harry Benjamin Collection, Kinsey Institute, Bloomington, IN.

77 Author concealed, 1975. "Letter from doctor to patient." Box 4, Harry Benjamin Collection, Kinsey Institute, Bloomington, IN.

78 Author concealed, 1972. "Letter from patient to Johns Hopkins Gender Identity Clinic." Box 3, Harry Benjamin Collection. Kinsey Institute. Bloomington, IN.

79 Irving (2008).

80 Harry Benjamin, 1958. "Letter to Doctor." Box 3, Harry Benjamin Collection, Kinsey Institute, Bloomington, IN.

81 Schweik (2009); Trent (1994).

82 Author concealed, 1969. "Letter from Doctor to Benjamin." Box 7, Harry Benjamin Collection, Kinsey Institute, Bloomington, IN.

83 Gamble (1997).

84 Schweik (2009).

85 Stubblefield (2007).

86 Markowitz (2001).

87 There are countless historical examples of how the authority of science has been used to mandate conformity to social norms. Historian Pablo Mitchell's (2005) work documented how invoking the "science" of bodily comportment justified the regulation of indigenous youth in New Mexico at the end of the 19th century. Indigenous youth were sent to boarding schools to isolate them from their families and maximize social control over their health, habits, behavior, culture, and languages. Historian David Serlin's (2004) work also shows how medical technologies and advancement in knowledge about "abnormal" bodies was used to further adherence to conformity in broader society.

88 H. Rubin (2006); Chauncey (1989).

89 Recent work by feminist science scholars Rebecca Jordan-Young and Katrina Karkazis (2019) analyzed the historical unfolding of endocrinology and the development of research on testosterone. As they suggested, "science" is often invoked to explain away behaviors that are marked as masculine. Through scientific misunderstandings, testosterone became popularized as the "male" hormone although most human bodies contain both estrogen and testosterone. C. Riley Snorton (2017) demonstrated how race is encoded in the medical establishment's handling of gender and, while often unacknowledged, racism influenced the development of the field of endocrinology.

2. LEGITIMACY WARS BETWEEN PHYSICIANS AND THERAPISTS

1 H. Rubin (2006).

2 Whooley (2019).

3 Benjamin (1967).

4 Benjamin (1967).

5 Harry Benjamin, 1968. "Letter from Benjamin to MD." Box 3, Harry Benjamin Collection, Kinsey Institute, Bloomington, IN.

6 Harry Benjamin, 1968. "Letter from Benjamin to MD." Box 3, Harry Benjamin Collection, Kinsey Institute, Bloomington, IN.

7 Author concealed, 1968. "Letter from doctor to Benjamin." Box 3, Harry Benjamin Collection, Kinsey Institute, Bloomington, IN.

8 Harry Benjamin, 1968. "Letter from Benjamin to physician." Box 3, Harry Benjamin Collection, Kinsey Institute, Bloomington, IN.

9 Whooley (2017).

10 Whooley (2019).

11 Rose (2004).

12 Whooley (2019).

13 The importance of diagnostic codes began to change in the late 1970s with the release of the *DSM-III*, which also signaled the first time that "gender identity disorder" appeared as a part of a formalized diagnostic classification system. Sociologist Annmarie Goldstein Jutel (2014) discusses the consequences of the diagnostic process in structuring the medical establishment and solidifying the authority of the mental health community.

14 Harry Benjamin, n.d. "Letter from Benjamin to doctor." Box 4, Harry Benjamin Collection, Kinsey Institute, Bloomington, IN.

15 Erickson Educational Foundation (1973).

16 While Harry Benjamin may have attempted to elevate the status of psychiatrists, he did not agree with the diagnosis of transsexualism as a form of schizophrenia. As he wrote to a medical provider in 1965, "It seems that the definition is by no means uniform, and that it is merely a label that explains absolutely nothing."

17 Author unknown, 1965. "Meeting of committee members of Erickson Foundation." Box 23, Harry Benjamin Collection, Kinsey Institute, Bloomington, IN.

18 Author unknown, 1965. "Meeting of committee members of the Erickson Foundation." Box 23, Harry Benjamin Collection, Kinsey Institute, Bloomington, IN.

19 Hollender and Hirsch (1964).

20 Brown (1980).

21 Author unknown, 1965. "Meeting of committee members of the Erickson Foundation." Box 23, Harry Benjamin Collection, Kinsey Institute, Bloomington, IN.

22 See also Spade (2006); Namaste (2005).

23 Author concealed, 1976. "Letter from psychologist to doctor." Box 7, Harry Benjamin Collection, Kinsey Institute, Bloomington, IN.

24 Rebecca Herzig's (2015) scholarship shows how hair removal practices were widely advocated as a means to help women achieve beauty standards for proper femininity around the beginning of the 20th century.

25 Author concealed, 1967. "Patient report from psychiatrist." Box 14, Harry Benjamin Collection, Kinsey Institute, Bloomington, IN.

26 Meyerowitz (2002); Stryker (2008).

27 Author unknown, 1968. "Clinical research." Box 14, Harry Benjamin Collection, Kinsey Institute, Bloomington, IN.

28 Author concealed, 1969. "Letter from psychiatrist to surgeon." Box 26, Harry Benjamin Collection, Kinsey Institute, Bloomington, IN.

29 Owen Whooley's (2019) work on diagnostic ambivalence documents the strategic workarounds that those in the mental health community have used to negotiate disagreements with formal diagnostic processes.
30 Author concealed, 1975. "Patient evaluation." Box 4, Harry Benjamin Collection, Kinsey Institute, Bloomington, IN.
31 Author concealed, 1962. "Letter from psychologist to Benjamin." Box 3, Harry Benjamin Collection, Kinsey Institute, Bloomington, IN.
32 Author concealed, 1976. "Letter from provider to surgeon." Box 3, Harry Benjamin Collection, Kinsey Institute, Bloomington, IN.
33 Erickson Educational Foundation (1973: 16–17).
34 De Block and Adriaens (2013); Hall (1992).
35 McWhorter (2009).
36 Erickson Educational Foundation (1973).
37 Light (2010).
38 Hacking (1990).
39 Author concealed, 1968. "Letter from psychologist to doctor." Box 7, Harry Benjamin Collection, Kinsey Institute, Bloomington, IN.
40 Benjamin (1967).
41 Stryker (2008).
42 Author concealed, 1966. "Letter from psychoanalyst to Benjamin." Box 24, Harry Benjamin Collection, Kinsey Institute, Bloomington, IN.
43 Author concealed, 1972. "Letter from Psychiatrist to Benjamin." Box 6, Harry Benjamin Collection, Kinsey Institute, Bloomington, IN.
44 At Johns Hopkins, for example, there was controversy in the late 1970s over the closure of the Gender Identity Clinic following a disputed publication from psychiatrists Jon Meyer and Donna Reter (1979). The authors concluded that while surgical interventions were cosmetically satisfactory, more importantly, trans patients continued to have difficulty with social adjustment in their target gender in job prospects, relationships, and creating a stable home life. This publication provoked intense debates within the medical establishment. While the publication was focused more on what happened to trans people after surgery, it also called into question the expertise of therapists and how success would be defined in therapeutic encounters. Eventually, the GIC at Johns Hopkins was closed. Psychologists associated with the GIC were disappointed, as they suggested in a press release in 1979 that the closing of the GIC "was a matter of medical morals, and not of scientific impartiality."
45 Hacking (1995).
46 Author concealed, 1973. "Letter from psychiatrist at the Stanford gender reorientation clinic to patient." Box 24, Harry Benjamin Collection, Kinsey Institute, Bloomington, IN.
47 Author concealed. 1975. "Letter from psychologist to doctor." Box 7, Harry Benjamin Collection, Kinsey Institute, Bloomington, IN.

48 As medical sociologist Daniel Chambliss (1996) has suggested in his work on the routinization of hospital care among nurses, one way that providers deal with ethical ambiguity in medical decision-making is to routinize healthcare delivery.

49 Erickson Educational Foundation (1971).

50 Author concealed, 1979. "Letter from director of counseling center to human services worker" Box 26, Harry Benjamin Collection, Kinsey Institute, Bloomington, IN.

51 Mara Buchbinder (2015) and Loren Wilbers (2015) separately analyze how stigma, once introduced into clinical encounters, is difficult for patients to work around.

52 Author concealed, n.d. "Case file." Box 9, Harry Benjamin Collection, Kinsey Institute, Bloomington, IN.

53 Baynton (2013).

54 Author unknown, 1966. "Harry Benjamin foundation meeting notes." Box 23, Harry Benjamin Collection, Kinsey Institute, Bloomington, IN.

55 Author unknown, 1965. "Meeting of committee members of Erickson Foundation." Box 23, Harry Benjamin Collection, Kinsey Institute, Bloomington, IN.

56 For readers unfamiliar with this term, "hoyden" refers to a boisterous girl.

57 Gender Identity Committee, 1967. "Meeting notes." Box 23, Harry Benjamin Collection, Kinsey Institute, Bloomington, IN.

58 Gender Identity Committee, 1967. "Meeting notes." Box 23, Harry Benjamin Collection, Kinsey Institute, Bloomington, IN.

59 Gender Identity Committee, 1967. "Meeting notes." Box 23, Harry Benjamin Collection, Kinsey Institute, Bloomington, IN.

60 Author concealed, 1964. "Letter from patient to Benjamin." Box 3, Harry Benjamin Collection, Kinsey Institute, Bloomington, IN.

61 Author concealed, 1964. "Letter from administrative assistant to patient." Box 3, Harry Benjamin Collection, Kinsey Institute, Bloomington, IN.

3. MAKING IT UP

1 Coleman (2013).

2 Timmermans and Kolker (2004).

3 Sociologists Wendy Espeland and Michael Sauder (2016) offer a rich discussion on the far-reaching consequences of rankings and standardization in social life.

4 Ruckenstein and Schüll (2017).

5 Timmermans and Berg (2003); Teston (2017).

6 Lambert, Gordon, and Bogdan-Lovis (2006).

7 As organizational scholars Paul DiMaggio and Walter Powell (1988) have documented, an efficient way to increase the legitimacy of decision-making when there are few established protocols is to mirror what peers are doing in other organizations or fields. Termed "isomorphism," this process shows how providers in emergent areas of medicine will likely look to more established areas for guidance in how to think about and act upon emergent areas of medicine.

8   Meyerowitz (2002); H. Rubin (2006).

9   Bakko and Kattari (2019).

10 The Board of Trustees for the State of North Carolina Health Plan voted in 2016 to include trans interventions but then reversed that decision on January 1, 2018, when the newly elected conservative Republican Dale Folwell staked his campaign for State Treasurer on removing "unnecessary spending" in the state health insurance plan (Iszler 2016). Trans coverage was a primary target in his campaign, although reports (see Segal Consulting 2016) indicated that trans coverage cost the average insurance plan participant between six and fifteen cents a year.

11 Conrad and Barker (2010).

12 Jutel (2009).

13 Brown (1995, 39).

14 Terry (1999).

15 Rottnek (1999).

16 Wake (2018).

17 Gonzales and Henning-Smith (2017).

18 Dewey and Gesbeck (2017).

19 Figert (2005).

20 Arnaud (2015).

21 Jutel (2014).

22 Bowker and Star (2000); Horwitz (2002).

23 Rebman et al. (2017).

24 Ray Blanchard's (1985) work on transsexualism is a prime example of the tendency for those in the medical community to use biologically essentialist ideas of sex to understand trans people.

25 World Health Organization (1992).

26 World Health Organization (2018).

27 Davis, Dewey, and Murphy (2016).

28 Grzanka, Zeiders, and Miles (2016).

29 Halperin (2012).

30 Link and Phelan (2001).

31 American Psychiatric Association (2012).

32 American Psychiatric Association (2013).

33 I examined all diagnostic categories in the *DSM-5* to make this claim.

34 Timmermans and Berg (2003).

35 Field notes, 2014, West coast trans healthcare conference.

36 The Endocrine Society guidelines have gained recognition in the medical community. In 2012, the American Psychiatric Association published a report applauding the work that the Endocrine Society undertook in creating a new set of guidelines (Byne et al. 2012). In the same report, the authors leveled a critique against the WPATH guidelines as not consistently meeting the Oxford Centre for

Evidence-Based Medicine's system for evaluating evidence. Ironically, neither do the Endocrine Society guidelines.

37 Dewey and Gesbeck (2017); shuster (2016).

38 Field notes, 2013, Midwestern trans health summit.

39 Field notes, 2015, East coast trans healthcare conference.

40 While clearly an important part of this conversation in how evidence is constructed in trans medicine, on the question of how youth are treated by the medical community, I refer readers to those scholars who have focused exclusively on this age range, as the medical community has different standards of care and guidelines for trans youth. See, for example, sociologist Travers's (2018) recent work on the medical establishment's handling of trans kids.

41 Previously it was a point of disagreement, but now almost all medical professional associations have publicly rejected the idea that conversion therapy works or is even an appropriate means for resolving gender dysphoria (Byne 2016).

42 Hembree et al. (2017).

43 Field notes, 2014, West coast trans healthcare conference.

44 Sociologist Kristin Barker's (2005) work on fibromyalgia documents the strategies medical providers use to uphold their medical authority when faced with an emergent area of medicine that lacks the tools for biologically testing the body to produce a verifiable result. Barker found that in response to confronting a patient population for whom they lacked a familiarity (and believability) with the symptoms, women's experiences were often relegated to the descriptor "psychosomatic."

45 According to the 2020 *Drugs of Abuse* resource guide issued by the Department of Justice's Drug Enforcement Agency, Schedule III drugs have a moderate-to-low potential for physical or psychological dependence. Other drugs in this category include anabolic steroids (which testosterone and estrogen are not) and ketamine. Because of its association with "steroids," testosterone is a Schedule III drug, which carries criminal penalties for misuse, while estrogen is not.

46 Field notes, 2015, East coast trans healthcare conference.

47 shuster (2018).

48 A1C refers to a blood test for glucose. This test is often used in the diagnostic process for prediabetes and type 2 diabetes. Medical consensus suggests that someone with 6.5 percent or above will likely have developed diabetes. Information accessed from the National Institute of Diabetes and Digestive and Kidney Diseases (2018). New research demonstrates there may be a correlation between taking estrogen and lowering the risk for developing type 2 diabetes (Pereira et al. 2015).

49 Timmermans and Epstein (2010).

50 Denzin (2009, 142).

51 Landsman (2006, 2672).

4. MEDICAL UNCERTAINTY

1 Barker (2005).

2 Meyerowitz (2002); Sanders and Rogers (2011).

3 While the medical community has not resolved this conflict, as trans people become more visible in public life, the narrative surrounding why people are trans remains within a biologically essentialist framing (Davis, Dewey, and Murphy 2016).

4 Landsman (2006).

5 Timmermans and Berg (2003).

6 These two strategies for using clinical guidelines—closely following or flexibly interpreting—are similar to those found elsewhere in the scholarship on medical decision-making. Stefan Timmermans and Alison Angell (2001) examined how pediatric residents interpreted EBM to manage uncertainty. They found that some residents consulted the literature as librarians, while others evaluated it critically. As they suggest, because the documents associated with EBM need to be interpreted, and not simply read for scientific facts, the strategies for managing EBM led to new kinds of uncertainty for medical residents.

7 Reich (2016).

8 As I described earlier, before the release of the *DSM-5*, gender dysphoria was listed under the diagnostic category for gender identity disorder. While the ICD uses "gender incongruence," for consistency, I use "gender dysphoria" to refer to the diagnostic category. This is a term used more frequently in the US, and all of the providers I interviewed and most of the providers I observed in healthcare conferences practiced medicine in the US. The World Professional Association for Transgender Health also uses the term "gender dysphoria."

9 Johnson (2015).

10 Garrison (2018); Serano ([2007] 2016); Stein (2018); Westbrook and Schilt (2014).

11 shuster (2016).

12 Pearce (2018).

13 Doan, Costa Candal, and Sylvester (2018).

14 The recent 2020 policy change to Section 1557 of the Affordable Care Act that removed recognition of gender identity as a basis for protection from discrimination is one such action the Trump administration has taken to undermine trans people and providers who offer trans medicine.

15 The length of time that trans people have to wait for receiving medical interventions has been described by sociologist Ruth Pearce (2018) as "trans time." As her work shows, slowing down the process helps providers feel assured, but can also be harmful to trans people who have to wait for prolonged periods of time to meet this expectation by the medical establishment. Further, many trans people have already expended a great deal of energy and thought over whether or not to physically transition before they raise the possibility with a medical provider.

16 Sociologist Travers (2018) similarly describes how slowing down a gender transition offers comfort to family members of trans youth who are grappling with uncertainty related to how a transition might shift the family dynamics, what a transition will mean for the family, and how others outside of the family will respond to physical and social changes.

17 Assimilating into cisgender culture is not a unidirectional process. As sociologist Kristen Schilt (2011) documented, many trans men who transition in the workplace enjoy masculine privilege. Part of that enjoyment is based on other people wanting to accommodate and affirm gender transitions through treating a trans man as "just one of the guys." But the trans men from her study do not necessarily resist this normative enculturation. Sociologist Catherine Connell (2010) showed how even when trans people attempt to resist binary gender norms, it is a difficult feat to accomplish because of the durability of other people's investments in upholding the gender binary.

18 Dewey (2015); Sumerau and Mathers (2019).

19 WPATH convened in the winter of 2019 to begin updating the guidelines for an 8th version to be released within the next few years.

20 Hembree et al. (2009).

21 Reich (2016).

5. UNCERTAIN EXPERTISE IN TRANS MEDICINE

1 There is ongoing discussion in endocrinology about what baseline to use for trans people on hormones. A recent special issue of *The Journal of Clinical Endocrinology & Metabolism*, for example, offered systemic reviews of published data. Many of the authors in the special issue concluded that the scientific evidence to make these determinations was inconclusive and therefore more data was recommended (see for example Maraka et al. 2017; Singh-Ospina et al. 2017).

2 Abbott (1988); Freidson (1971).

3 Timmermans and Berg (2003).

4 Ridgeway (2011).

5 Preserving a trans person's sperm or eggs is becoming a more frequent topic of conversation between medical providers and trans patients (Martin 2010), disrupting the historically common practice of sterilizing trans people either through removal of the gonads or through the introduction of large doses of estrogen or testosterone. However, freezing and preserving eggs and sperm is also prohibitively expensive for trans people, many of whom are under- or unemployed, compared to their cisgender counterparts (Bakko and Kattari 2019; Streed, McCarthy, and Haas 2017).

6 Hacking (1986); Heidegger (1962); Latour and Woolgar (2013); Streeck and Mehus (2005).

7 Jutel (2010).

8 Nettleton (2006).

9 Dreger (2000).

10 Eric Plemons's (2017) recent work on facial feminization surgery for trans women details how surgeons and trans people are moving away from emphasizing genital-based surgical interventions. This new emphasis and constitution of gender through facial surgery was not apparent in the trans healthcare conferences I observed, nor reflected in the presentations from surgeons who specialized in other areas of plastic surgery.

11 Goffman (1959).

12 Salamon (2010).

13 The connection between transgender and amputation surgical requests has been an ongoing controversy since the early 2000s. Some of the more well-known scholars who have written about these connections are Anne Lawrence and Sheila Jeffreys. While this debate is outside the parameters of this chapter, for those interested readers, please see Jeffreys (2014); Lawrence (2006). For counter arguments see Nichols (2008). For historical contexts of this connection, grounded in feminist theories, see Stryker and Sullivan (2009).

14 Valentine (2007).

15 Foucault (1995).

16 Rubin et al. (2018).

17 Anthony, Campos-Castillo, and Lim (2018).

18 Knight and Mattick (2006).

19 Chambliss (1996).

20 Spade (2006: 319).

CONCLUSION

1 Green, Benner, and Pear (2018).

2 Bakko and Kattari (2019); Cruz (2014); Gonzales and Henning-Smith (2017); Streed, McCarthy, and Haas (2018).

3 For example, on June 12, 2020, the administration negated a previous ruling on Section 1557 of the Affordable Care Act, which had outlined gender identity as a protected category. Led by Health and Human Services, this change did not result in a federal definition of gender. It effectively erased trans and nonbinary people from federal policy. As the ruling from HHS (2020) suggested, it intended to interpret sex as, "according to the plain meaning of the word 'sex' as male or female and as determined by biology." The interpretation by HHS has since been stayed following the *Bostock v. Clayton County* ruling by the Supreme Court that banned discrimination based on sexual orientation or gender identity just three days after the HHS attempted to erase protections for trans people in the ACA (Keith 2020). Clearly, this is a quickly changing landscape that will likely shift again. The future of the ACA is uncertain and there will likely be more changes in the coming months and before this book makes its way into print.

4 shuster (2017) offers an analysis of how language acts as a form of discursive violence against trans and nonbinary people in institutional settings and everyday life.

5 Centers for Disease Control and Prevention (2020).

6 Reich (2016); Suryanarayanan and Kleinman (2016).

7 Pape (2019).

8 Fausto-Sterling (2000).

9 Menchik (2014).

10 Landsman (2006).

11 Kamm, Thelen, and Jensen (1990).

12 Landsman (2006).

13 Espeland and Sauder (2016).

14 Robertson (2006).

15 Harding (1991).

16 Stubblefield (2007).

17 Grosz (1994: x).

18 Douglas (1980); Kristeva (1982).

19 Davis, Dewey, and Murphy (2016); Paine (2018).

20 McCright and Dunlap (2003); Oreskes and Conway (2010).

21 Reich (2016).

APPENDIX

1 Franzosi (1998: 548).

2 Sociologist Steven Epstein's (1994) work details the development of sociological research on sexuality. As he describes, the first wave of queer research in sociology, while sometimes in opposition to the methodological conventions that Kinsey used because they did not pass social scientific muster, built on Kinsey's classic work (1948; 1953) on male and female sexuality.

3 Bullough (1998); Bancroft (2004).

4 Bancroft (2004).

5 I made multiple trips to the Kinsey Institute archives over several years to examine various collections related to transgender medicine, healthcare providers, and trans people. Because of time limitations, I did not examine every folder in each collection that might have trans-related materials. Sometimes a folder in a specific collection contained a single letter of correspondence. Others contained longer histories across three to ten years. For the more extensive collections (those holding more than 50 folders), I examined every third file folder that appeared in the collection.

6 Psychologist Rebecca Campbell's (2002) work on the impact of studying sexual assault victims on researchers is a rare exception to this observation.

7 A representative sample was not possible because as an emergent field, trans medicine is not coherently organized as a specialization with specific licensing or educational tracks. But the sample does represent a diverse range of providers' perspectives and experiences working in this medical arena.

8 Lofland, Anderson, and Lofland (2006).

REFERENCES

Abbott, Andrew. 1988. *The System of Professions*. Chicago: University of Chicago Press.

Abelson, Miriam. 2019. *Men in Place: Trans Masculinity, Race, and Sexuality in America*. Minneapolis: University of Minnesota Press.

Aizura, Aren Z. 2016. "Affective Vulnerability and Transgender Exceptionalism." In *Trans Studies: The Challenge to Hetero/Homo Normativities*, edited by Y. Martinez-San Miguel and S. Tobias, 122–141. New Brunswick, NJ: Rutgers University Press.

American Psychiatric Association. 2012. Press release: Gender Dysphoria. www.psychiatry.org.

———. 2013. *Diagnostic and Statistical Manual of Mental Disorders*, 5th edition. Arlington, VA: American Psychiatric Association.

Anthony, Denise L., Celeste Campos-Castillo, and Paulina Lim. 2018. "Who Isn't Using Patient Portals and Why? Evidence and Implications From a National Sample of US Adults." *Health Affairs* 37(12).

Armstrong, Elizabeth M. 2003. *Conceiving Risk, Bearing Responsibility: Fetal Alcohol Syndrome and the Diagnosis of Moral Disorder*. Baltimore: Johns Hopkins University Press.

Arnaud, Sabine. 2015. *On Hysteria: The Invention of a Medical Category Between 1670 and 1820*. Chicago: University of Chicago Press.

Bakko, Matthew, and Shanna K. Kattari. 2019. "Differential Access to Transgender Inclusive Insurance and Healthcare in the United States: Challenges to Health across the Life Course." *Journal of Aging & Social Policy*. https://doi.org/10.1080/08959420.2019.1632681.

Bancroft, John. 2004. "Alfred C. Kinsey and the Politics of Sex Research." *Annual Review of Sex Research* 15(1): 1–39.

Barker, Kristin. 2005. *The Fibromyalgia Story: Medical Authority and Women's Worlds of Pain*. Philadelphia: Temple University Press.

Baynton, Douglas. 2013. "Disability and the Justification of Inequality in American History." In *The Disability Studies Reader*, edited by L. Davis, 33–57. New York: Routledge.

Benjamin, Harry. 1967. "Transvestism and Transsexualism in the Male and Female." *Journal of Sex Research* 3(2): 107–127.

Berger, Peter L., and Thomas Luckmann. 1967. *The Social Construction of Reality: A Treatise in the Sociology of Knowledge*. New York: Anchor Books.

Bergstrand, Kelly, and James Jasper. 2018. "Villains, Victims, and Heroes in Character Theory and Affect Control Theory." *Social Psychology Quarterly* 81(3): 228–247.

Bettcher, Talia Mae. 2007. "Evil Deceivers and Make-Believers: On Transphobic Violence and the Politics of Illusion." *Hypatia* 22: 43–65.

Blanchard, Ray. 1985. "Typology of Male-to-Female Transsexualism." *Archives of Sexual Behavior* 14: 247–261.

Bosk, Charles. [1979] 2003. *Forgive and Remember: Managing Medical Failure.* Chicago: University of Chicago Press.

Bostock v. Clayton County, 590 U.S. ___ (2020).

Bowker, Geoffrey, and Susan Leigh Star. 2000. *Sorting Things Out: Classification and Its Consequences.* Cambridge, MA: MIT Press.

Breuer, Josef, and Sigmund Freud. [1900] 2000. *Studies on Hysteria.* Translated by James Strachey. New York: Basic Books.

Brookes-Howell, Lucy Claires. 2006. "Living Without Labels: The Interactional Management of Diagnostic Uncertainty in the Genetic Counseling Clinic." *Social Science & Medicine* 63: 3080–3091.

Brown, Phil. 1980. "Social Implications of Deinstitutionalization." *Journal of Community Psychology.* 8(4): 314–322.

———. 1995. "Naming and Framing: The Social Construction of Diagnosis and Illness." *Journal of Health and Social Behavior* 35: 34–52.

Buchbinder, Mara. 2015. *All In Your Head: Making Sense of Pediatric Pain.* Oakland: University of California Press.

Bullough, Vern L. 1998. "Alfred Kinsey and the Kinsey Report: Historical Overview and Lasting Contributions." *Journal of Sex Research* 35: 127–131.

Busch, Lawrence. 2011. *Standards: Recipes for Reality.* Cambridge, MA: MIT Press.

Butler, Judith. 1993. *Bodies that Matter: On the Discursive Limits of Sex.* New York: Routledge.

Byne, William, Susan J. Bradley, Eli Coleman, A. Evan Eyler, Richard Green, Edgardo J. Menvielle, Heino F. L. Meyer-Bahlburg, Richard R. Pleak, and Andrew Tompkins. 2012. "Report of the American Psychiatric Association Task Force on Treatment of Gender Identity Disorder." *Archives of Sexual Behavior* 41(4): 759–796.

Campbell, Rebecca. 2002. *Emotionally Involved: The Impact of Researching Rape.* New York: Routledge.

Casper, Monica. J. 1998. *The Making of the Unborn Patient: A Social Anatomy of Fetal Surgery.* New Brunswick, NJ: Rutgers University Press.

Castañeda, Claudia. 2015. "Developing Gender: The Medical Treatment of Transgender Young People." *Social Science & Medicine* 143: 262–270.

Centers for Disease Control and Prevention. 2020. "People at Increased Risk and Other People Who Need to Take Extra Precautions." www.cdc.gov.

Chambliss, Daniel. F. 1996. *Beyond Caring: Hospitals, Nurses, and the Social Organization of Ethics.* Chicago: University of Chicago Press.

Chauncey, George. 1989. "From Sexual Inversion to Homosexuality: The Changing Medical Conceptualization of Female Deviance." *Passion and Power: Sexuality in History* 109: 1890–1940.

Cioffi, Jane. 2000. "Nurses' Experiences of Making Decisions to Call Emergency Assistance to Their Patients." *Journal of Advanced Nursing* 32(1): 108–114.

Cipolla, Cyd, Kristina Gupta, David A. Rubin, and Angela Willey, editors. 2017. *Queer Feminist Science Studies*. Seattle: University of Washington Press.

Coleman, Eli. 2013. "WPATH's Standards of Care for the Health of Transsexual, Transgender, and Gender Nonconforming People: Version 7—An Overview." Plenary presented at the National Transgender Health Summit, Oakland, CA, May 18.

Connell, Catherine. 2010. "Doing, Undoing, or Redoing Gender? Learning from the Workplace Experiences of Transpeople." *Gender & Society* 24(1): 31–55.

Conrad, Peter. 1992. "Medicalization and Social Control." *Annual Review of Sociology* 18: 209–232.

———. 2007. *The Medicalization of Society: On the Transformation of Human Conditions into Medical Disorders*. Baltimore: Johns Hopkins University Press.

Conrad, Peter, and Kristin K. Barker. 2010. "The Social Construction of Illness: Key Insights and Policy Implications." *Journal of Health and Social Behavior* 51: S67–S79.

Coontz, Stephanie. [1992] 2016. *The Way We Never Were: American Families and the Nostalgia Trap*. New York: Basic Books.

Cromwell, Jason. 1999. *Transmen and FTMs: Identities, Bodies, Genders, and Sexualities*. Chicago: University of Illinois Press.

Cruz, Taylor M. 2014. "Assessing Access to Care for Transgender and Gender Nonconforming People: A Consideration of Diversity in Combating Discrimination." *Social Science & Medicine* 110: 65–73.

Davis, Georgiann. 2015. *Contesting Intersex: The Dubious Diagnosis*. New York: New York University Press.

Davis, Georgiann, Jodie M. Dewey, and Erin L. Murphy. 2016. "Giving Sex: Deconstructing Intersex and Trans Medicalization Practices." *Gender & Society* 30(3): 490–514.

Davis, Lennard J. 1995. *Enforcing Normalcy: Disability, Deafness, and the Body*. New York: Verso.

De Block, Andreas, and Pieter R. Adriaens. 2013. "Pathologizing Sexual Deviance: A History." *Journal of Sex Research* 50(3–4): 276–298.

Denzin, Norman K. 2009. "The Elephant in the Living Room: Or Extending the Conversation About the Politics of Evidence." *Qualitative Research* 9(2): 139–160.

Deutsch, Madeline. n.d. "Overview of Masculinizing Hormone Therapy." Center of Excellence for Trans Health. transhealth.ucsf.edu. Accessed September 1, 2018.

Dewey, Jodie M. 2015. "Challenges of Implementing Collaborative Models of Decision Making with Trans-Identified Patients." *Health Expectations* 18(5): 1508–1518.

Dewey, Jodie M., and Melissa M. Gesbeck. 2017. "(Dys)Functional Diagnosing: Mental Health Diagnosis, Medicalization, and the Making of Transgender Patients." *Humanity & Society* 41(1): 37–72.

DiMaggio, Paul J., and Walter W. Powell. 1998. "The Iron Cage Revisited: Institutional Isomorphism and Collective Rationality in Organizational Fields." *American Sociological Review* 48: 147–161.

Doan, Alesha, Carolina Costa Candal, and Steven Sylvester. 2018. "'We Are the Visible Proof': Legitimizing Abortion Regret Misinformation through Activists' Experiential Knowledge." *Law & Policy* 40(1): 33–56.

Douglas, Mary. 1980. *Purity and Danger: An Analysis of the Concepts of Pollution and Taboo.* London: Routledge.

———. 1986. *How Institutions Think.* Syracuse, NY: Syracuse University Press.

Dreger, Alice D. 2000. *Hermaphrodites and the Medical Invention of Sex.* Cambridge, MA: Harvard University Press.

Epstein, Steven. 1994. "A Queer Encounter: Sociology and the Study of Sexuality." *Sociological Theory* 12(2): 188–202.

———. 1998. *Impure Science: AIDS, Activism, and the Politics of Knowledge.* Berkeley: University of California Press.

Erickson Educational Foundation. 1971. *An Outline of Medical Management of the Transexual: Endocrinology, Surgery, Psychiatry.* Baton Rouge, LA: Erickson Educational Foundation.

———. 1973. *Counseling the Transexual Five Conversations with Professionals in Transexual Therapy.* Baton Rouge, LA: Erickson Educational Foundation.

Eskridge, William N. Jr. 1999. *Gaylaw: Challenging the Apartheid of the Closet.* Cambridge, MA: Harvard University Press.

Espeland, Wendy, and Michael Sauder. 2016. *Engines of Anxiety: Academic Rankings, Reputation, and Accountability.* New York: Russell Sage Foundation.

Fausto-Sterling, Anne. 2000. *Sexing the Body: Gender Politics and the Construction of Sexuality.* New York: Basic Books.

Feinberg, Leslie. 1997. *Transgender Warriors: Making History from Joan of Arc to Dennis Rodman.* Boston: Beacon Press.

Figert, Anne E. 2005. "Premenstrual Syndrome as Scientific and Cultural Artifact." *Integrative Physiological & Behavioral Science* 40(2): 102–113.

Flores, Andrew, Jody L. Herman, Gary J. Gates, and Taylor N. Brown. 2016. "How Many Adults Identify as Transgender in the United States?" Williams Institute, UCLA. williamsinstitute.law.ucla.edu.

Fordyce, Lauren. 2013. "Accounting for Fetal Death: Vital Statistics and the Medicalization of Pregnancy in the United States." *Social Science & Medicine* 92: 124–131.

Foucault, Michel. [1963] 1994. *The Birth of the Clinic: An Archaeology of Medical Perception.* London: Routledge.

———. 1995. *Discipline & Punish: The Birth of the Prison.* New York: Vintage.

Fox, Renée C. 1959. *Experiment Perilous: Physicians and Patients Facing the Unknown.* Glencoe, IL: Free Press.

Franzosi, Roberto. 1998. "Narrative Analysis—Or Why (and How) Sociologists Should Be Interested in Narrative." *Annual Review of Sociology* 24: 517–554.

Freidson, Eliot. 1971. *The Profession of Medicine: A Study of the Sociology of Applied Knowledge.* New York: Dodd, Mead.

Gamble, Vanessa Northington. 1997. "Under the Shadow of Tuskegee: African-Americans and Health Care." *American Journal of Public Health* 87(1): 1773–1778.

Garland-Thomson, Rosemarie. 1997. *Extraordinary Bodies: Figuring Physical Disability in American Culture and Literature*. New York: Columbia University Press.

Garrison, Spencer. 2018. "On the Limits of 'Trans Enough': Authenticating Trans Identity Narratives." *Gender & Society* 32(5): 613–637.

Gerrity, Martha S., Jo Anne L. Earp, Robert F. DeVellis, and Donald W. Light. 1992. "Uncertainty and Professional Work: Perceptions of Physicians in Clinical Practice." *American Journal of Sociology* 97: 1022–1051.

Ghosh, Amit Kumar. 2004. "On the Challenges of Using Evidence-Based Medicine: The Role of Clinical Uncertainty." *Journal of Lab Clinical Medicine* 144: 60–64.

Giffort, Danielle M., and Kelly Underman. 2016. "The Relationship Between Medical Education and Trans Health Disparities: A Call to Research." *Sociology Compass* 10(11): 999–1013.

Goffman, Erving. 1959. *The Presentation of Self in Everyday Life*. New York: Anchor Books.

Gonzales, Gilbert, and Carrie Henning-Smith. 2017. "Barriers to Care Among Transgender and Gender Nonconforming Adults." *Milbank Quarterly* 95(4): 726–748.

Green, Erica L., Katie Benner, and Robert Pear. 2018. "Transgender Could be Defined Out of Existence Under Trump Administration." *New York Times*. October 21.

Grosz, Elizabeth. 1994. *Volatile Bodies: Toward a Corporeal Feminism*. Bloomington: Indiana University Press.

Grzanka, Patrick R., Katharine H. Zeiders, and Joseph R. Miles. 2016. "Beyond 'Born this Way?' Reconsidering Sexual Orientation Beliefs and Attitudes." *Journal of Counseling Psychology* 63(1): 67–75.

Hacking, Ian. 1986. "Making Up People." In *Reconstructing Individualism: Autonomy, Individuality and the Self in Western Thought*, edited by T. C. Heller, 222–236. Stanford, CA: Stanford University Press.

———. 1990. *The Taming of Chance*. Cambridge: Cambridge University Press.

———. 1995. "The Looping Effect of Human Kinds" In *Causal Cognition: A Multidisciplinary Debate*, edited by D. Sperber, D. Premack, and A. J. Premack, 351–383. Oxford: Oxford University Press.

Hall, Lesley A. 1992. "Forbidden by God, Despised By Men: Masturbation, Medical Warnings, Moral Panic, and Manhood in Great Britain, 1850–1950." *Journal of the History of Sexuality* 2(3): 365–387.

Halperin, David M. 2012. *How to Be Gay*. Cambridge, MA: Harvard University Press.

Haraway, Donna. 1991. *Simians, Cyborgs, and Women: The Reinvention of Nature*. New York: Routledge.

Harding, Sandra. 1991. *Whose Science? Whose Knowledge? Thinking from Women's Lives*. Ithaca, NY: Cornell University Press.

———. 2008. *Sciences from Below: Feminisms, Postcolonialities, and Modernities*. Durham, NC: Duke University Press.

Hausman, Bernice. 1995. *Changing Sex: Transsexualism, Technology, and the Idea of Gender*. Durham, NC: Duke University Press.

Health and Human Services. 2020. "Press Release: HHS Finalizes Rule On Section 1557 Protecting Civil Rights in Healthcare, Restoring the Rule of Law, and Relieving Americans of Billions in Excessive Costs." June 12. www.hhs.gov.

Heidegger, Martin. 1962. *Being and Time*. New York: Harper & Row.

Hembree, Wylie, Peggy Cohen-Kettenis, Henriette Delemarre-van de Waal, Louis J. Gooren, Walter Myer III, Norman Spack, Vin Tangpricha, and Victor M. Montori. 2009. "Endocrine Treatment of Transsexual Persons: An Endocrine Society Clinical Practice Guidelines." *Journal of Clinical Endocrinology and Metabolism* 94: 3132–3154.

Hembree, Wylie, Peggy Cohen-Kettenis, Louis Gooren, Sabine E. Hannema, Walter J. Meyer, M. Hassan Murad, Stephen M. Rosenthal, Joshua D. Safer, Vin Tangpricha, Guy G. T'Sipen. 2017. "Endocrine Treatment of Gender Dysphoric/Gender-Incongruent Persons: An Endocrine Society Clinical Practice Guideline." *Journal of Clinical Endocrinology and Metabolism* 102(11): 3869–3903.

Herzig, Rebecca. 2015. *Plucked: A History of Hair Removal*. New York: New York University Press.

Hirschfeld, Magnus. 1910. *Transvestites: The Erotic Drive to Cross-Dress*. Brooklyn, NY: Prometheus Books.

Hollender, Marc H., and Steven J. Hirsch. 1964. "Hysterical Psychosis." *American Journal of Psychiatry* 120(11): 1066–1074.

Horwitz, Allan. 2002. *Creating Mental Illness*. Chicago: University of Chicago Press.

Irving, Dan. 2008. "Normalized Transgressions: Legitimizing the Transsexual Body as Productive." *Radical History Review* 100: 38–59.

Irwig, Michael. 2017. "Testosterone Therapy for Transgender Men." *Lancet Diabetes & Endocrinology* 5(4): 301–311.

Iszler, Madison. 2016. "NC Health Plan to Cover Sex Changes, If Medically Necessary, in 2017." *News & Observer*. December 7. www.newsobserver.com.

Jeffreys, Sheila. 2014. *Beauty and Misogyny: Harmful Cultural Practices of the West*. New York: Routledge.

Johnson, Austin. 2015. "Normative Accountability: How the Medical Model Influences Transgender Identities and Experiences." *Sociology Compass* 9(9): 803–813.

Jordan-Young, Rebecca M., and Katrina Karkazis. 2019. *Testosterone: An Unauthorized Biography*. Cambridge, MA: Harvard University Press.

Jorgensen, Christine. [1967] 2000. *Christine Jorgensen: A Personal Autobiography*. San Francisco: Cleis Press.

Jutel, Annemarie. 2009. "Sociology of Diagnosis: A Preliminary Review." *Sociology of Health & Illness* 31: 279–299.

———. 2010. "Medically Unexplained Symptoms and the Disease Label." *Social Theory and Health*. 8(3): 229–245.

———. 2014. *Putting a Name to It: Diagnosis in Contemporary Society*. Baltimore: Johns Hopkins University Press.

Kamm, Kathi, Esther Thelen, and Jody L. Jensen. 1990. "A Dynamical Systems Approach to Motor Development." *Physical Therapy* 70(12): 763–775.

Karkazis, Katrina. 2008. *Fixing Sex: Intersex, Medical Authority, and Lived Experience.* Durham, NC: Duke University Press.

Keith, Katie. 2020. "Court Vacates New 1557 Rule that Would Roll Back Antidiscrimination Protections for LBGT Individuals." *Health Affairs Blog.* www.healthaffairs. org.

Kinsey, Alfred C., Wardell B. Pomeroy, and Clyde E. Martin. 1948. *Sexual Behavior in the Human Male.* Philadelphia: Saunders.

Kinsey, Alfred C., Wardell B. Pomeroy, Clyde E. Martin, and Paul H. Gebhard. 1953. *Sexual Behavior in the Human Female.* Philadelphia: Saunders.

Knight, Lynn Valerie, and Karen Mattick. 2006. "'When I First Came Here, I Thought Medicine Was Black and White': Making Sense of Medical Students' Ways of Knowing." *Social Science & Medicine* 63(4): 1084–1096.

Kristeva, Julia 1982. *Powers of Horror: An Essay on Abjection.* Translated by Leon Roudiez. New York: Columbia University Press.

Lambert, Helen, Elisa J. Gordon, and Elizabeth A. Bogdan-Lovis. 2006. "Introduction: Gift Horse or Trojan Horse? Social Science Perspectives on Evidence-Based Health Care." *Social Science & Medicine* 62(11): 2613–2620.

Landsman, Gail H. 2006. "What Evidence, Whose Evidence?: Physical Therapy in New York State's Clinical Practice Guideline and in the Lives of Mothers and Disabled Children." *Social Science & Medicine* 62: 2670–2680.

Laqueur, Thomas. 1992. *Making Sex: Body and Gender from the Greeks to Freud.* Cambridge, MA: Harvard University Press.

Latour, Bruno. 1993. *We Have Never Been Modern.* Cambridge, MA: Harvard University Press.

Latour, Bruno, and Steve S. Woolgar. 2013. *Laboratory Life: The Construction of Scientific Facts.* Princeton, NJ: Princeton University Press.

Lawrence, Anne. 2006. "Clinical and Theoretical Parallels Between Desire for Limb Amputation and Gender Identity Disorder." *Archives of Sexual Behavior* 35(3): 263–278.

Light, Donald. 2010. "Health-Care Professions, Markets, and Countervailing Powers." In *The Handbook of Medical Sociology*, edited by C. E. Bird, P. Conrad, A. Fremont, and S. Timmermans, 270–289. Nashville, TN: Vanderbilt University Press.

Link, Bruce G., and Jo C. Phelan. 2001. "Conceptualizing Stigma." *Annual Review of Sociology* 27: 363–384.

———. 2014. "Stigma Power." *Social Science & Medicine* 103: 24–32.

Lofland, John, David Snow, Leon Anderson, and Lyn H. Lofland. 2006. *Analyzing Social Settings: A Guide to Qualitative Observations and Analysis*, 4th edition. Belmont, CA: Wadsworth.

Maraka, Spyridoula, Naykky Singh Ospina, Rene Rodriguez-Gutierrez, Caroline J. Davidge-Pitts, Todd B. Nippoldt, Larry J. Prokop, and M. Hassan Murad. 2017. "Sex Steroids and Cardiovascular Outcomes in Transgender Individuals: A Systematic Review and Meta-analysis." *Journal of Clinical Endocrinology & Metabolism* 102(11): 3914–3923.

Markowitz, Sally. 2001. "Pelvic Politics: Sexual Dimorphism and Racial Difference." *Signs: Journal of Women in Culture and Society* 26(2): 389–414.

Martin, Lauren Jade. 2010. "Anticipating Infertility: Egg Freezing, Genetic Preservation, and Risk." *Gender.& Society* 24(4): 526–545.

McCright, Aaron M., and Riley E. Dunlap. 2003. "Defeating Kyoto: The Conservative Movement's Impact on U.S. Climate Change Policy." *Social Problems* 50: 348–373.

McKinlay, John B. and Lisa D. Marceau 2002. "The End of the Golden Age of Doctoring." *International Journal of Health Services* 32: 379–416.

McWhorter, Ladelle. 2009. *Racism and Sexual Oppression in Anglo-America: A Genealogy.* Bloomington: Indiana University Press.

Menchik, Daniel. 2014. "Decisions About Knowledge in Medical Practice: The Effect of Temporal Features of a Task." *American Journal of Sociology* 120(3): 701–749.

Meyer, Jon K., and Donna J. Reter. 1979. "Sex Reassignment: Follow-up." *Archives of General Psychiatry* 36(9): 1010–1015.

Meyerowitz, Joanne. 2002. *How Sex Changed: A History of Transexuality.* Cambridge, MA: Harvard University Press.

Mishel, Merle H. 1990. "Reconceptualization of Uncertainty in Illness Theory." 22(4): 256–262.

Mitchell, Pablo. 2005. *Coyote Nation: Sexuality, Race, and Conquest in Modernizing New Mexico, 1880–1920.* Chicago: University of Chicago Press.

Mol, Annemarie. 2003. *The Body Multiple: Ontology in Medical Practice.* Durham, NC: Duke University Press.

Money, John, Joan G. Hampson, and John L. Hampson. "An Examination of Some Basic Sexual Concepts: The Evidence of Human Hermaphroditism." *Bulletin of the Johns Hopkins Hospital* 97(4): 301–319.

Namaste, Viviane. 2005. *Sex Change, Social Change: Reflections on Identity, Institutions, and Imperialism.* Toronto: Women's Press.

National Institute of Diabetes and Digestive and Kidney Diseases. 2018. "The A1C Test & Diabetes." www.niddk.nih.gov.

Nettleton, Sarah. 2006. "'I Just Want Permission to be Ill': Towards a Sociology of Medically Unexplained Symptoms." *Social Science & Medicine* 62(5): 1167–1178.

Nichols, Margaret. 2008. "Dreger on the Bailey Controversy: Lost in the Drama, Missing the Big Picture." *Archives of Sexual Behavior* 37: 476–480.

Obedin-Maliver, Juno, Elizabeth S. Goldsmith, Leslie Stewart, William White, Eric Tran, Stephanie Brenman, Maggie Wells, David M. Fetterman, Gabriel Garcia, and Mitchell R. Lunn. 2011. "Lesbian, Gay, Bisexual, and Transgender–related Content in Undergraduate Medical Education." *JAMA* 306(9): 971–977.

Oreskes, Naomi, and Erik M. Conway. 2010. *Merchants of Doubt: How a Handful of Scientists Obscured the Truth on Issues from Tobacco Smoke to Climate Change.* New York: Bloomsbury Press.

Paine, Emily A. 2018. "Embodied Disruption: 'Sorting Out' Gender and Nonconformity in the Doctor's Office." *Social Science & Medicine* 211: 352–358.

Pape, Madeleine. 2019. "Expertise and Non-binary Bodies: Sex, Gender, and the Case of Dutee Chand." *Body & Society* 25(4): 3–28.

Parsons, Talcott. 1951. *The Social System*. Glenco, IL: Free Press.

Pearce, Ruth. 2018. *Understanding Trans Health, Discourse, Power, and Possibility*. Bristol, UK: Policy Press.

Pereira, Rosa I., Beth A. Casey, Tracy A. Swibas, Collin B. Erickson, Phillip Wolfe, and Rachael E. Van Pelt. 2015. "Timing of Estradiol Treatment after Menopause May Determine Benefit or Harm to Insulin Action." *Journal of Clinical Endocrinology & Metabolism* 100(12): 4456–4462.

Pescosolido, Bernice A., and Carol A. Boyer. 2001. "The American Health Care System: Entering the Twenty-First Century with High Risk, Major Challenges, and Great Opportunities." In *The Blackwell Companion to Medical Sociology*, edited by W. C. Cockerham, 180–198. Oxford: Blackwell.

Plemons, Eric. 2017. *The Look of a Woman: Facial Feminization Surgery and the Aims of Trans Medicine*. Durham, NC: Duke University Press.

Politi, Mary C., Paul K. J. Han, and Nananda F. Col. 2007. "Communicating the Uncertainty of Harms and Benefits of Medical Interventions." *Medical Decision Making* 27(5): 681–695.

Poteat, Tonia, Danielle German, and Deanna Kerrigan. 2013. "Managing Uncertainty: A Grounded Theory of Stigma in Transgender Health Care Encounters." *Social Science & Medicine* 84: 22–29.

Prosser, Jay. 1998. *Second Skins: The Body Narrative of Transsexuality*. New York: Columbia University Press.

Rebman, Alison W., John N. Aucott, Eric R. Weinstein, Kathleen T. Bechtold, Katherine C. Smith, and Lori Leonard. 2017. "Living in Limbo: Contested Narratives of Patients with Chronic Symptoms Following Lyme Disease." *Qualitative Health Research* 27(4): 534–546.

Reich, Jennifer A. 2016. *Calling the Shots: Why Parents Reject Vaccines*. New York: New York University Press.

Ridgeway, Cecilia. 2011. *Framed by Gender: How Gender Inequality Persists in the Modern World*. New York: Oxford University Press.

Robertson, Steve. 2006. "'I've Been Like a Coiled Spring This Last Week': Embodied Masculinity and Health." *Sociology of Health and Illness* 28(4): 433–446.

Rose, Nikolas. 2004. "Becoming Our Neurochemical Selves." In *Biotechnology, Commerce and Civil Society*, edited by N. Stehr, 89–128. Edison, NJ: Transaction Publishers.

Rottnek, Matthew. 1999. *Sissies and Tomboys: Gender Nonconformity and Homosexual Childhood*. New York: New York University Press.

Rubin, David A. 2012. "'An Unnamed Blank That Craved a Name': A Genealogy of Intersex as Gender." *Signs: Journal of Women in Culture and Society* 37(4): 909–933.

Rubin, Henry. 2006. "The Logic of Treatment." In *The Transgender Studies Reader*, edited by S. Stryker and S. Whittle, 482–498. New York: Routledge.

Rubin, Sara, Nancy Burke, Meredith Van Natta, Irene Yen, Irene, and Janet K. Shim. 2018. "Like a Fish out of Water: Managing Chronic Pain in the Urban Safety Net." *Journal of Health and Social Behavior* 59(4): 487–500.

Ruckenstein, Minna, and Natasha Dow Schüll. 2017. "The Datafication of Health." *Annual Review of Anthropology* 46: 261–278.

Sackett, David L., William M. C. Rosenberg, J. A. Gray, Brian R. Haynes, and W. Scott Richardson. 1996. "Evidence Based Medicine: What It Is and What It Isn't." *British Medical Journal* 312: 71–72.

Salamon, Gayle. 2010. *Assuming a Body: Transgender Rhetorics of Materiality*. New York: Columbia University Press.

Sanders, Caroline, and Anne Rogers. 2011. "Bodies in Context: Potential Avenues of Inquiry for the Sociology of Chronic Illness and Disability Within a New Policy Era." In *Handbook of the Sociology of Health, Illness, and Healing: A Blueprint for the 21st Century*, edited by B. Pescosolido, J. Martin, J. McLeod, and A. Rogers, 483–504. New York: Springer.

Schilt, Kristen. 2011. *Just One of the Guys? Transgender Men and the Persistence of Gender Inequality*. Chicago: University of Chicago Press.

Schweik, Susan Marie. 2009. *The Ugly Laws: Disability in Public*. New York: New York University Press.

Scott, Joan W. 1986. "Gender: A Useful Category of Historical Analysis." *The American Historical Review*. 91(5): 1053–1075.

Segal Consulting. 2016. "Transgender Cost Estimate Memorandum." November 29.

Serano, Julia. [2007] 2016. *Whipping Girl: A Transsexual Woman on Sexism and the Scapegoating of Femininity*, 2nd edition. Berkeley, CA: Seal Press.

Serlin, David. 1995. "Christine Jorgensen and the Cold War Closet." *Radical History Review* 62: 136–165.

———. 2004. *Replaceable You: Engineering the Body in Postwar America*. Chicago: University of Chicago Press.

shuster, stef. 2016. "Uncertain Expertise and the Limitations of Clinical Guidelines in Transgender Healthcare." *Journal of Health and Social Behavior* 57(3): 319–32.

———. 2017. "Punctuating Accountability: How Discursive Aggression Regulates Transgender People." *Gender & Society* 31(4): 481–502.

———. 2018. "Passing as Experts in Transgender Medicine." In *After Marriage Equality: The Unfinished Queer Agenda*, edited by A. Jones, J. DeFilippis, and M. Yarbrough, 74–87. New York: Routledge.

———. 2019. "Performing Informed Consent in Transgender Medicine." *Social Science & Medicine*. 226: 190–197.

Singh-Ospina, Naykky, Spyridoula Maraka, Rene Rodriguez-Gutierrez, Caroline Davidge-Pitts, Todd B. Nippoldt, Larry J. Prokop, and Mohammad Hassan Murad. 2017. "Effect of Sex Steroids on the Bone Health of Transgender Individuals: A Systematic Review and Meta-analysis." *Journal of Clinical Endocrinology & Metabolism* 102(11): 3904–3913.

Snorton, C. Riley. 2017. *Black on Both Sides: A Racial History of Trans Identity*. Minneapolis: University of Minnesota Press.

Spade, Dean. 2006. "Mutilating Gender." In *The Transgender Studies Reader*, edited by S. Stryker and S. Whittle, 315–332. New York: Routledge.

Stark, Laura. 2012. *Behind Closed Doors: IRBs and the Making of Ethical Research*. Chicago: University of Chicago Press.

Starr, Paul. [1982] 2017. *The Social Transformation of American Medicine: The Rise of a Sovereign Profession and the Making of a Vast Industry*. New York: Basic Books.

Stein, Arlene. 2018. *Unbound: Transgender Men and the Remaking of Identity*. New York: Pantheon.

Streeck, Jürgen, and Siri Mehus. 2005. "Microethnography: The Study of Practices." In *The Handbook of Language and Social Interaction*, edited by K. Finch & R. E. Sanders, 381–402. Mahwah, NJ: Lawrence Erlbaum Associates.

Streed, Carl G. Jr., Ellen P. McCarthy, and Jennifer S. Haas. 2018. "Self-reported Physical and Mental Health of Gender Nonconforming Transgender Adults in the United States." *LGBT Health* 5(7): 443–448.

Stryker, Susan. 2008. *Transgender History*. Berkeley, CA: Seal Press.

Stryker, Susan, and Nikki Sullivan. 2009. "King's Member, Queen's Body: Transsexual Surgery, Self-Demand Amputation and the Somatechnics of Sovereign Power." In *Somtechnics: Queering the Technologisation of Bodies*, edited by N. Sullivan and S. Murray, 49–64. Burlington, VT: Ashgate.

Stubblefield, Anna. 2007. "Beyond the Pale: Tainted Whiteness, Cognitive Disability, and Eugenic Sterilization." *Hypatia* 22(2): 162–181.

Sumerau, J. E., and Lain A. B. Mathers. 2019. *America Through Transgender Eyes*. Lanham, MD: Rowman & Littlefield.

Suryanarayanan, Sainath, and Daniel Lee Kleinman. 2016. *Vanishing Bees: Science, Politics, and Honeybee Health*. New Brunswick, NJ: Rutgers University Press.

Sweet, Paige L., and Claire Laurier Decoteau. 2018. "Contesting Normal: The DSM-5 and Psychiatric Subjectivation." *Biosocieties* 13: 103–122.

Terry, Jennifer. 1999. *An American Obsession: Science, Medicine, and Homosexuality in Modern Society*. Chicago: University of Chicago Press.

Teston, Christa. 2017. *Bodies in Flux: Scientific Methods for Negotiating Medical Uncertainty*. Chicago: University of Chicago Press.

Timmermans, Stefan, and Alison Angell. 2001. "Evidence-Based Medicine, Clinical Uncertainty, and Learning to Doctor." *Journal of Health and Social Behavior* 42(4): 342–359.

Timmermans, Stefan, and Marc Berg. 2003. *The Gold Standard: The Challenge of Evidence-Based Medicine and Standardization in Health Care*. Philadelphia: Temple University Press.

Timmermans, Stefan, and Steven Epstein. 2010. "A World of Standards But Not a Standard World: Toward a Sociology of Standards and Standardization." *Annual Review of Sociology* 36: 69–89.

Timmermans, Stefan, and Emily Kolker. 2004. "Evidence-Based Medicine and the Reconfiguration of Medical Knowledge." *Journal of Health and Social Behavior* 45: 177–193.

Timmermans, Stefan, and Hyeyoung Oh. 2010. "The Continued Social Transformation of the Medical Profession." *Journal of Health and Social Behavior* 51: S94–S106.

Timmermans, Stefan, Ashelee Yang, Melissa Gardner, Catherine E. Keegan, Beverly M. Yashar, Patricia Y. Fechner, Margarett Shnorhavorian, Eric Vilain, Laura A. Siminoff, and David E. Sandberg. 2018. "Does Patient-Centered Care Change Genital Surgery Decisions? The Strategic Use of Clinical Uncertainty in Disorders of Sex Development Clinics." *Journal of Health and Social Behavior* 59(4): 520–535.

Travers, A. 2018. *The Trans Generation: How Trans Kids (and Their Parents) Are Creating a Gender Revolution*. New York: New York University Press.

Trent, James. 1994. *Inventing the Feeble Mind: A History of Mental Retardation in the United States*. Berkeley: University of California Press.

Underman, Kelly. 2015. "Playing Doctor: Simulation in Medical School as Affective Practice." *Social Science & Medicine* 136: 180–188.

Valentine, David. 2007. *Imagining Transgender: An Ethnography of a Category*. Durham, NC: Duke University Press.

Wake, Naoko. 2018. "Homosexuality and Psychoanalysis Meet at a Mental Hospital: An Early Institutional History." *Journal of the History of Medicine and Allied Sciences* 74(1): 34–56.

Westbrook, Laurel, and Kristen Schilt. 2014. "Doing Gender, Determining Gender: Transgender People, Gender Panics, and the Maintenance of the Sex/Gender/Sexuality System." *Gender & Society* 28(1): 32–57.

Whooley, Owen. 2017. "Defining Mental Disorders: Sociological Investigations into the Classification of Mental Disorders." In *A Handbook for the Study of Mental Health: Social Contexts, Theories, and Systems*, vol. 3, edited by T. Scheid and E. R. Wright, 45–64. Cambridge: Cambridge University Press.

———. 2019. *On the Heels of Ignorance: Psychiatry and the Politics of Not Knowing*. Chicago: University of Chicago Press.

Wilbers, Loren. 2015. "She Has a Pain Problem, Not a Pill Problem: Chronic Pain Managements, Stigma, and the Family—An Autoethnography." *Humanity & Society* 39(1): 86–111.

Winnick, Terri. 2005. "From Quackery to 'Complementary Medicine': The American Medical Profession Confronts Alternative Medicine." *Social Problems* 52: 73–97.

World Health Organization. 1992. *International Classification of Diseases*, 10th revision. Salt Lake City, Utah.

———. 2018. *International Classification of Diseases*, 11th revision. icd.who.int.

World Professional Association for Transgender Health. 2012. *Standards of Care for the Health of Transsexual, Transgender, and Gender-Nonconforming People*, 7th version.

INDEX

Abbott, Andrew, 7
abortions, 107
activism, x, 84–85
advocacy, 165
Affordable Care Act, 197n14, 199n3
American Medical Association (AMA), 23–26
American Psychiatric Association (APA), vii, 13, 82–85, 178, 183, 195n36
anatomy, 135–36
Angell, Alison, 197n6
anti-vaccination movement, 165–66
APA. *See* American Psychiatric Association
appearance, 38, 57
archival work, 175–78
Armstrong, Elizabeth M., 10
assessment, 6, 17, 50, 54–55, 57–60
Association for Voluntary Sterilization, 47
attractiveness, 37–38
authority: with exams, 147; in healthcare, 53–54, 165–66; medical, 8–11; in medical community, 127–28; for patients, 145; from professionalism, 118; of providers, 24, 44–46, 163; of science, 41, 191n87; for therapists, 123–24. *See also* decision-making

bathrooms, 132
behavioral therapy, 53–54
Benjamin, Harry, 15, 24, 26–30, 177, 187n1; with doctors, 51; model citizens

for, 44, 46; paternalism of, 44; with patients, 33–34, 38; with providers, 46–47, 54; psychiatry for, 73, 192n16; on science, 41–42; surgery for, 32–33, 36–37, 39–40
Berger, Peter, 13
Bettcher, Talia Mae, 31
binary gender expression, 142, 162, 198n17
binary gender identification, 114–17
bioethics, 135, 195n24, 197n3
bioindicators, 81–82, 96
biomedical psychiatry, 54–55
Blue Cross Blue Shield, 80
Bostock v. Clayton County, 199n3
Brookes-Howell, Lucy, 8

cancer, 94
CEUs. *See* continuing education units
challenges, 3–4, 93–94, 110–11, 126, 138
Chambliss, Daniel, 194n48
childhood, 31, 71–72
cisgender culture, 198n17
citizens, model, 16–17, 25, 34, 68, 127, 177; for Benjamin, 43–44, 46
classifications, 53–55, 66–68
classificatory looping, 66, 68
climate change, 165
clinical experience, 130–31, 137, 144; evidence and, 101; expertise from, 7, 18; gut instincts and, 79, 126–27, 158; learning on the job and, 4; for providers, 107; of therapists, 124

ABOUT THE AUTHOR

stef m. shuster is Assistant Professor of Sociology at Michigan State University.

CPSIA information can be obtained
at www.ICGtesting.com
Printed in the USA
JSHW042115220822
29538JS00002B/2